Student Workbook

Aviation Maintenance Technician Handbook

FAA-H-8083-30B

General

Production Staff

Designer/Photographer Dustin Blyer
Senior Designer/Production Manager Roberta Byerly
Contributor David Jones
Editor Jeff Strong

International Standard Book Number 1-933189-62-2
ISBN 13: 978-1-933189-62-8
Order # T-FAA-H-8083-30B-0102

For Sale by: Avotek
A Select Aerospace Industries, Inc. company

Mail to:
P.O. Box 219
Weyers Cave, VA 24486
USA

Ship to:
200 Packaging Drive
Weyers Cave, VA 24486
USA

Toll Free: 800-828-6835
Telephone: 540-234-9090
Fax: 540-234-9399

First Edition
Fifth Printing
Printed in the USA

www.avotek.com

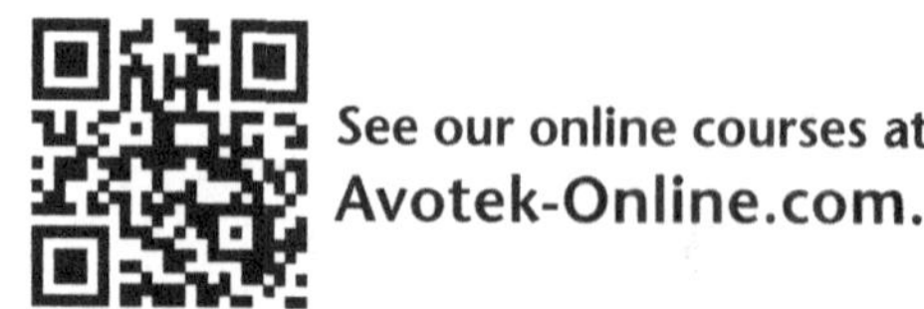

Contents

To the Student

This student workbook accompanies *Aviation Maintenance Technician Handbook–General*, FAA-H-8083-30 versions A and B, the first in a three book series. This workbook should be used as a tool for highlighting the strengths and pinpointing the weaknesses of the AMT student gathering the skill and knowledge necessary to build a strong foundation in the aircraft maintenance field. Specifically, it evaluates the progress made in applicable subject areas.

The foundation on which this workbook has been built assumes that the student is actively engaged in preparing for two goals: the first is to pass all required testing for the FAA Airframe and Powerplant Mechanic Certificate, and the second is to obtain the necessary skills and knowledge to function as an entry-level mechanic in the field. Both goals must be kept in mind and the material presented here has been designed to maintain that balance.

Each chapter of the text is divided into three different question formats and printed on perforated sheets for removal and presentation. They are presented as follows:

Fill in the Blank

These questions are designed to help the student understand new terminology and fundamental facts essential to the understanding of section material.

Multiple Choice

These questions offer a broader overview of the material by offering several possible answers, and allowing the student to identify the correct answer either through recognition or through the process of elimination.

Analysis

These are complex questions that require the student to access information presented in the text, analyze the data, and record a response. Successful completion of the analysis questions shows the student has a thorough understanding of the material in the chapter.

The answers for each set of questions are available from your course instructor. ➤

Avotek® Textbook Library

FILL IN THE BLANK
QUESTIONS

name:

date:

1. In every shop, signs should be posted to indicate dangerous or hazardous conditions and to indicate the location of first aid and _________________ equipment.

2. Two factors affect safety when dealing with electricity: fear and _________________.

3. Never use _________________ to clean your hands, as it can force debris into your skin and lead to infection.

4. The _________________ on a Material Safety Data Sheet shows the relative risk of a material.

5. The first safety rule for using a drill press, lathe, milling machine, or other high-speed-revolution equipment is to wear _________________.

6. A/An _________________ creates an area of low pressure in front of it that will draw in any loose object and propel it great distances, with force, out the other side.

7. A fire requires three things: fuel, heat, and _________________.

8. _________________ fire extinguishers are used for Class A, B, and C fires, but should not be used on a Class D fire.

9. The most effective extinguisher for a Class D fire is _________________.

10. An airplane should be tied down headed as nearly as possible _________________, depending on the locations of the available fixed tiedown points.

11. When starting an aircraft engine, a/an _________________, someone equipped with a fire extinguisher and familiar with aircraft starting procedures, should be stationed next to the outboard side of the engine, in view of the pilot.

12. Before starting a radial engine that has been shut off for more than 30 minutes, check that the ignition switch is off and then turn the propeller three or four revolutions by hand to check for a/an _________________.

13. When hand cranking an engine with no self-starter, the person turning the propeller first calls out (to the person operating the engine): "Fuel on, switch off, _________________, brakes on."

14. In case of a fire while starting an engine, the CO_2 from the fire extinguisher should be directed into the engine's _________________.

15. Usually, the first step in starting a turboprop engine is to turn the _________________ on.

16. The _________________ indicator is an instrument in a turbofan aircraft that measures the ratio between turbine inlet pressure and outlet pressure.

FILL IN THE BLANK QUESTIONS

name:

date:

17. ________________________ are smaller turbine engines that provide compressed air for starting engines, cabin heating and cooling, and electrical power while the aircraft is on the ground.

18. Before an aircraft is towed, a qualified person must be in the cockpit to ________________________ in the event that the tow bar fails or becomes unhooked.

19. An aircraft should be ________________________ immediately after it is parked in a hangar.

20. The standard position for a signalman directing an aircraft is slightly ahead of the aircraft and in line with the aircraft's ________________________.

21. The oil level in a turbine engine should be checked just after ________________________.

22. Because of fire danger, aircraft should not be serviced with ________________________ during fueling, defueling, or other maintenance work.

23. The two types of aviation fuel in general use are aviation gasoline, known as AVGAS, and ________________________, also known as JET A fuel.

24. Fuel flowing through a fuel line and an aircraft moving through the air both cause ________________________ to build.

25. Smaller aircraft are usually fueled through fueling ports located ________________________.

1. When inflating tires on any type of aircraft wheels, always use:
   a. Tire cage guards
   b. A hand pump
   c. Appropriate lifting and mounting devices
   d. Electronic tire sensors

2. The red portion of a Material Safety Data Sheet risk diamond indicates:
   a. Hazard
   b. Health
   c. Reactivity
   d. Flammability

3. The yellow portion of a Material Safety Data Sheet risk diamond indicates:
   a. Hazard
   b. Health
   c. Reactivity
   d. Flammability

4. Three of the blocks in a Material Safety Data Sheet risk diamond contain a number. What numbers are used and what number indicates the greatest risk?
   a. 0 through 10, with 0 indicating the greatest risk
   b. 0 through 4, with 4 indicating the greatest risk
   c. 0 through 4, with 0 indicating the greatest risk
   d. 0 through 5, with 5 indicating the greatest risk

5. Which of the following safety procedures does not apply to working on a drill press?
   a. Ground the metal that you are going to drill
   b. Wear eye protection
   c. Securely clamp all work
   d. Stop the machine before attempting to remove jammed work

6. Which of these instructions should be kept in mind when approaching a helicopter?
   a. Never approach a single-rotor helicopter from the rear.
   b. Always go from one side of a helicopter to the other by going around the rear.
   c. Always go from one side of a helicopter to the other by going around the nose.
   d. Both A and C.

7. A fire that involves energized electrical wiring and equipment is classified as:
   a. Class A
   b. Class B
   c. Class C
   d. Class D

8. A fire that involves combustible materials like wood, cloth, or paper is classified as:
   a. Class A
   b. Class B
   c. Class C
   d. Class D

9. A fire that involves flammable petroleum products like solvents or paint is classified as:
   a. Class A
   b. Class B
   c. Class C
   d. Class D

10. Water extinguishers are only recommended for use on what type of fire?
    a. Class A
    b. Class B
    c. Class C
    d. Class D

11. A device frozen or buried in ice or snow in order to secure a ski plane is called a:
    a. Bowline
    b. Tiedown loop
    c. Chock
    d. Dead man

Chapter 1
Safety, Ground Operations, and Servicing

MULTIPLE CHOICE QUESTIONS

name:

date:

MULTIPLE CHOICE
QUESTIONS

name:

date:

12. Positioning an aircraft to head into the prevailing wind prior to starting its engines helps to:
    a. Ensure proper takeoff position
    b. Provide sufficient airflow over the engines for cooling
    c. Make it easier to move the aircraft based on the tower's orders
    d. Remove debris from the intake area

13. To eliminate a hydraulic lock in a reciprocating engine:
    a. Remove the front or rear spark plug from the lower cylinder and pull the propeller through.
    b. Pull the propeller through in the direction opposite to normal rotation.
    c. Force the propeller to turn through the lock.
    d. Open the throttle to a position that will provide 1,000 to 1,200 rpm.

14. The primary cause of backfiring when starting a hand-cranking engine is:
    a. Gradual opening of the throttle
    b. A faulty switch that controls the magnetos
    c. Excessive throttle opening
    d. Overpriming the engine

15. Which of these statements best describes the starting sequence for a turbine engine?
    a. The igniters are turned on to spark the fuel; the main compressor is turned on; the engine accelerates to self-sustaining speed and the starter is disengaged
    b. The starter turns the main compressor; at the correct speed, the igniters are turned on and the fuel is lit; the engine accelerates to self-sustaining speed and the starter is disengaged
    c. The switch and throttle are engaged; compressors are turned on; the propeller levers are activated
    d. The ignition switch is turned on; the aircraft boost pumps are turned on; the start switch is placed in "start" position; the engine accelerates to idle speed

16. On a turbine engine, a hot start occurs when:
    a. The engine starts normally, but the rpm remains at a low rate rather than increasing to the normal starting rate.
    b. The engine will not start within the prescribed time limit.
    c. The engine starts, but the exhaust gas temperature exceeds specified limits.
    d. Insufficient electrical power is provided to the ignition system.

17. On a large aircraft like the one illustrated in Figure 1-17, the engine exhaust hazard area at idle speed:
    a. Extends 200 feet behind the engine, at which point exhaust gases can be 100°F and travel at 35 knots
    b. Extends 150 feet behind the engine, at which point exhaust gases can be 100°F and travel at 100 knots
    c. Extends 100 feet behind the engine, at which point exhaust gases can be 300°F and travel at 200 knots
    d. Extends 100 feet behind the engine, at which point exhaust gases can be 100°F and travel at 25 knots

18. The towing speed of an aircraft should not exceed:
    a. 5 miles per hour
    b. 10 miles per hour
    c. 25 miles per hour
    d. The speed of walking team members

19. A flashing red taxi signal light means:
    a. Stop
    b. Taxi clear of the runway in use
    c. Return to starting point
    d. Exercise extreme caution

Safety, Ground Operations, and Servicing

20. The standard hand taxi signal for "start engines" is:
    a. A circular motion with the right hand while pointing 45 degrees upward with the left hand
    b. Moving both hands from the person's sides toward the person's body
    c. Flapping both hands up and down
    d. Crossing both hands above the person's head

21. Electric ground power units can supply which of the following?
    a. Battery power to start light aircraft
    b. Variable-voltage direct current for starting turbine engines
    c. Constant-voltage direct current for starting reciprocating engines
    d. All the above

MULTIPLE CHOICE
QUESTIONS

22. Which type of commercially available oxygen is the only one that should be used in cabin air systems?

name:

    a. Industrial oxygen
    b. Aviator's breathing oxygen
    c. Medical oxygen
    d. Any of these is acceptable

date:

23. In 100/130 grade AVGAS, the rich mixture octane rating is:
    a. 50
    b. 100
    c. 130
    d. 65

24. What can happen if AVGAS is added to jet fuel?
    a. Engine power decreases and the engine will be damaged or detonate.
    b. The two fuels are interchangeable—nothing will happen.
    c. Lead deposits can form in the turbine engine and reduce service life.
    d. The mixed fuel can combine with oil, grease, or bituminous material to form a highly explosive mixture.

25. The fueling method in which a receptacle on the bottom of the leading edge of the wing is used to fill all the fuel tanks on the aircraft is called:
    a. Over-the-wing fueling
    b. Single-point fueling
    c. Static-avoidance fueling
    d. Pressure fueling

1. How can a technician's mental attitude toward electricity create or diminish safety hazards?

2. Describe the arrangement of a material safety diamond and what the contents of it can tell a technician.

3. What makes machine tools like drill presses, lathes, milling machines, and grinders potentially hazardous? What steps can make them less hazardous?

4. What are some sources of noise on the flight line or hangar, what is the danger of noise to the technician, and how can that danger be prevented?

Chapter 1
Safety, Ground Operations, and Servicing

ANALYSIS
QUESTIONS

name:

date:

Chapter 1
Safety, Ground Operations, and Servicing

ANALYSIS
QUESTIONS

name:

date:

5. Fire requires three things: fuel, heat, and oxygen. How do water and carbon dioxide fire extinguishers work to remove one or more of these ingredients and thus stop a fire? On what types of fires are these extinguishers effective, and on what types of fire can they be dangerous?

6. How do you tie down a light aircraft?

7. Describe the basic steps in starting a reciprocating engine.

8. What are some avoidable errors that occur in servicing aircraft fluids?

9. Describe the common grades of aviation gasoline and turbine fuel. How are they identified?

10. What are some things that can contaminate fuel, what are their effects, and how can fuel contamination be avoided?

<u>Chapter 1</u>

Safety, Ground Operations, and Servicing

ANALYSIS
QUESTIONS

name:

date:

Chapter 2

Regulations, Maintenance Forms, Records, and Publications

FILL IN THE BLANK
QUESTIONS

name:

date:

1. The FAA regulations that govern today's aircraft are found in Title _______________ of the *Code of Federal Regulations*.

2. There are 75 federal regulations related to aircraft separated into the three volumes that cover administrative matters, airworthiness certification, and _______________.

3. The FAA sometimes issues _______________, which are focused on a specific situation and are usually effective for only a limited time.

4. According to the FAA, "airworthy" means the aircraft conforms to its _______________ and is in a condition for safe operation.

5. The group within the FAA that a maintenance technician has the most interaction with is the _______________.

6. 14 CFR Part _______________ identifies the requirements of and procedures for obtaining certification for products and parts.

7. Part 23 aircraft are those with a maximum certificated takeoff weight of _______________ or less (or 19,000 pounds or less for commuter aircraft).

8. 14 CFR Part _______________ details the type certificate requirements for reciprocating and turbine aircraft engines.

9. 14 CFR Part 43 provides the standards for _______________ all civilian aircraft registered in the United States.

10. Although 14 CFR Part _______________ deals with general operating and flight rules and is primarily aimed at owners, operators, and pilots, maintenance technicians should be familiar with this regulation.

11. A/An _______________ is an operation that advertises itself as willing to transport people or property from place to place for compensation.

12. The curriculum you must take at an aviation maintenance technical school is designed in accordance with 14 CFR Part _______________, Appendix A.

13. A propeller, for example, that has been disassembled, cleaned, inspected, repaired, reassembled, and tested to the same tolerances and limits as a new propeller is said to have been _______________.

14. Returning an aircraft to service after major repair or alteration requires a _______________ that includes the use of FAA Form 337, Major Repair and Alteration.

FILL IN THE BLANK
QUESTIONS

name:

date:

15. A certificated repairman is authorized to work on a product undergoing maintenance but is not authorized to approve the product for _____________________.

16. A/An _____________________ part is any part for which a mandatory replacement limit has been specified.

17. If an inspecting technician rejects an item being inspected for a return to service, a list of _____________________ must be given to the aircraft owner as described in 14 CFR section 43.11, paragraph (b).

18. According to 14 CFR Part 91, all maintenance performed on an aircraft must be done in accordance with Part 43 and in compliance with the appropriate manufacturer maintenance manuals and _____________________.

19. A/An _____________________ inspection is a visual examination or check of an item, but does not require disassembly.

20. _____________________ of 14 CFR Part 43 describes the scope and detail of annual and 100-hour inspections.

21. A "411 test," which covers the _____________________ system, each altimeter instrument, and each automatic pressure altitude reporting system, must be performed at least every 24 months.

22. Testing of the ATC transponder system, required every _____________________, is commonly referred to as the "413 test."

23. _____________________ may still be needed as a reference for aircraft first certificated in the 1940s, 1950s, and 1960s.

24. Good parts with bad paperwork and bad parts with "good" (but actually bogus) paperwork fall into the category of _____________________.

25. The contents of _____________________ are not binding unless incorporated into a regulation by reference; rather, they are issued to provide guidance and information in a designated subject area or to show a method acceptable to the FAA for complying with a relation federal aviation regulation.

26. _____________________ are issued by the FAA and require that the relevant problem must be corrected on all aircraft or aircraft parts using the same design.

27. A/An _____________________ is a document issued by the FAA approving an aircraft, engine, or propeller modification. It defines the design change, states how the modification affects the existing type design, and lists the serial numbers affected.

28. A/An _________________________ is a formal description of an aircraft, engine, or propeller that lists the specifications, conditions, and limitations under which airworthiness requirements are met for the product, such as engine make and model, fuel type, engine limits, airspeed limits, maximum weight, minimum crew, and more.

29. A Supplemental Type Certificate number that begins with "SE" indicates that the document is a Supplemental Type Certificate for _________________________.

30. An aircraft's Instructions for Continued Airworthiness must contain a section called "_________________________" that states mandatory replacement times, structural inspection intervals, and related inspection procedures.

31. FAA Form 8130-6 is an application for _________________________.

32. To apply for a/an _________________________, you can download and print the proper form. The aircraft owner can mail in a completed copy and keep a copy of the form as temporary authority to operate the aircraft.

33. A radio station license is required if an aircraft is equipped with radios and will be flown _________________________ of the United States.

Chapter 2
Regulations, Maintenance Forms, Records, and Publications

FILL IN THE BLANK QUESTIONS

name:

date:

1. Which of these categories is not regulated under 14 CFR?
   a. The National Aeronautics and Space Administration
   b. The Department of Transportation
   c. Aircraft
   d. Air quality

2. In regulatory materials, the word "product" refers to:
   a. An aircraft
   b. An aircraft engine
   c. An aircraft propeller
   d. A, B, or C

3. Which of these is not a member of the three primary regulations that govern the airworthiness of an aircraft?
   a. 14 CFR Part 21, Certification Procedures for Products and Parts
   b. 14 CFR Part 43, Maintenance, Preventive Maintenance, Rebuilding, and Alterations
   c. 14 CFR Part 39, Airworthiness Directives
   d. 14 CFR Part 91, General Operating and Flight Rules

4. Which of these describes airworthiness standards for commuter airplanes?
   a. 14 CFR Part 29
   b. 14 CFR Part 23
   c. 14 CFR Part 25
   d. 14 CFR Part 27

5. Which of these describes airworthiness standards for most commercial aircraft?
   a. 14 CFR Part 29
   b. 14 CFR Part 23
   c. 14 CFR Part 25
   d. 14 CFR Part 27

6. Which of these describes airworthiness standards for turbine-style aircraft engines?
   a. 14 CFR Part 29
   b. 14 CFR Part 33
   c. 14 CFR Part 35
   d. 14 CFR Part 39

7. When an airworthiness directive is printed in the Federal Register, it is considered an amendment to which of these?
   a. 14 CFR Part 29
   b. 14 CFR Part 33
   c. 14 CFR Part 35
   d. 14 CFR Part 39

8. Replacement and modification parts must be marked with "FAA-PMA" and other information. "PMA" indicates:
   a. Proper Modification Authority
   b. Private Monitoring Agency
   c. Parts Manufacturing Approval
   d. Parts Manufacturing Agent

9. Which of these people are certificated under 14 CFR Part 65?
   a. Mechanics
   b. Pilots
   c. Flight crew
   d. Ground instructors

10. Large, for-hire private carriage aircraft operations are conducted under which of these?
    a. 14 CFR Part 91
    b. 14 CFR Part 125
    c. 14 CFR Part 121
    d. 14 CFR Part 135

11. Records from repair station maintenance activity must be retained for a minimum of:
    a. 6 months
    b. 1 year
    c. 2 years
    d. 5 years

12. The requirements for obtaining a maintenance training certificate are described in:
    a. 14 CFR Part 65
    b. 14 CFR Part 135
    c. 14 CFR Part 147
    d. 14 CFR Part 183

<u>Chapter 2</u>

Regulations, Maintenance Forms, Records, and Publications

MULTIPLE CHOICE QUESTIONS

name:

date:

MULTIPLE CHOICE QUESTIONS

name:

date:

13. Which of these people is not authorized under 14 CFR Part 43 to perform maintenance?
   a. Aircraft owner
   b. Certified mechanic
   c. Holder of repair station certificate
   d. Certified repairman

14. Which of these people is not authorized under 14 CFR Part 43 to approve an aircraft for return to service?
   a. Certificated private pilot
   b. The manufacturer
   c. Holder of repair station certificate
   d. Holder of Part 135 certificate

15. Which of these must appear in a maintenance record entry?
   a. The name of the person who did the work
   b. A description of the work performed
   c. The date the work was performed
   d. All the above are required

16. The accumulated cycles, hours, or any other mandatory limit of a life-limited part is referred to as the part's:
   a. Life story
   b. Life status
   c. Type certificate
   d. Life station

17. Falsification of aircraft records—a potentially dangerous act—is dealt with in:
   a. 14 CFR section 43.11
   b. 14 CFR section 91.410
   c. 14 CFR section 43.12
   d. CAR 3

18. Which of the following accurately describes the differences between an annual inspection and a 100-hour inspection?
   a. The list of items and areas to be inspected are exactly the same, and the only difference is who is authorized to return the aircraft to service following the inspection.
   b. The list of items and areas to be inspected in an annual inspection is considerably longer and more in depth than the list for a 100-hour inspection.
   c. The list of items and areas to be inspected in a 100-hour inspection is longer and more in depth than the list for an annual inspection.
   d. The list of items and areas to be inspected in a 100-hour inspection has very little overlap with the list of items and areas to be inspected in an annual inspection.

19. Which of these regulations states that "no person may operate a civil aircraft unless it is in an airworthy condition"?
   a. 14 CFR Part 43
   b. 14 CFR Part 91
   c. 14 CFR Part 21
   d. 14 CFR Part 129

20. A 100-hour inspection can be postponed by as much as 10 hours of flight time if the aircraft is en route to the inspection facility. If an airplane has flown 105 hours since its last 100-hour inspection, how many hours can it fly before the next 100-hour inspection is due?
   a. 100 hours
   b. 105 hours
   c. 95 hours
   d. The next inspection is performed at the owner/operator's discretion.

21. Who is authorized to perform a 411 test and calibration of the altimeter system?
   a. The aircraft manufacturer, a properly rated repair station, or a certificated airframe mechanic
   b. Only a certificated airframe mechanic
   c. A properly rated repair station, a certificated airframe mechanic, or an appropriately rated test pilot
   d. The aircraft manufacturer or a properly rated repair station

<u>Chapter 2</u>

Regulations, Maintenance Forms, Records, and Publications

MULTIPLE CHOICE
QUESTIONS

name:

date:

22. An aircraft engine rebuilt by the engine manufacturer:
    a. May be given a new maintenance record, showing no previous operating history
    b. Must include previous operating history in its maintenance records
    c. Requires an entirely new type certificate data sheet
    d. Can only be serviced by the engine manufacturer

23. The first federal legislation to regular civil aviation was enacted in:
    a. 1954
    b. 1963
    c. 1938
    d. 1926

24. Which of these aircraft is certified under CAR 3?
    a. Gulfstream 1159
    b. Cessna 140 seaplane
    c. Cessna 182
    d. Piper PA 37

25. Which of these documents are used to inform the aviation public in a systematic way of non-regulatory material?
    a. Airworthiness Directives
    b. Advisory Circulars
    c. Supplemental Type Certificates
    d. Instructions for Continued Airworthiness

26. Which of these documents are issued by the FAA to require action to correct deficiencies or unsafe conditions found in aircraft, engines, propellers, or aircraft parts?
    a. Airworthiness Directives
    b. Advisory Circulars
    c. Supplemental Type Certificates
    d. Instructions for Continued Airworthiness

27. A (theoretical) airworthiness directive numbered 2011-2-03 was issued:
    a. in December 2011
    b. in June 2011
    c. in March 2011
    d. in January 2011

28. Which of these documents is issued by the FAA to approve a product modification and to describe how the modification affects the existing type design?
    a. Airworthiness Directives
    b. Advisory Circulars
    c. Supplemental Type Certificates
    d. Instructions for Continued Airworthiness

29. A Special Airworthiness Certificate can be issued to which of these classes of aircraft?
    a. Utility
    b. Manned Free Balloon
    c. Acrobatic
    d. Light-Sport

30. Which of these statements regarding maintenance record entries is true?
    a. 14 CFR section 43.9 requires the technician to make appropriate entries of maintenance actions in the aircraft maintenance record.
    b. 14 CFR section 43.10 requires the technician to make appropriate entries of inspection results in the aircraft maintenance record.
    c. 14 CFR section 91.418 requires that maintenance records be kept by the owner until the work is repeated, superseded, or one year has elapsed.
    d. All the above are true.

MULTIPLE CHOICE
QUESTIONS

name:

date:

31. The first complete set of aircraft industry–consensus standards developed by a non-government agency (namely, the American Society for Testing and Materials) cover the design, manufacture and use of:
    a. Acrobatic aircraft
    b. Light-sport aircraft
    c. Environmentally friendly aircraft
    d. Hobby kit aircraft

32. Which of the following is considered "heavy" maintenance, repair, or alteration of an LSA aircraft?
    a. Repainting the control surfaces
    b. Patching a hole in fabric
    c. Installation of a strobe light kit
    d. Replacing the battery

1. Under what circumstances are aircraft not required to meet current design regulations? What type of FAA publication takes precedence over current design regulations and must be adhered to by all affected aircraft?

2. Of the three primary regulations that govern the airworthiness of an aircraft, which ones have to do with maintenance or recurrent airworthiness?

3. What are some topics covered in the "airworthiness standards" regulations for general aviation, commercial aviation, and helicopters? How do the regulations define general aviation and commercial aviation aircraft?

Chapter 2

Regulations, Maintenance Forms, Records, and Publications

ANALYSIS QUESTIONS

name:

date:

ANALYSIS
QUESTIONS

name:

date:

4. What are the three primary regulations that govern the airworthiness of an aircraft? Provide a summary of the content of each one.

5. What information is required on a fireproof data plate or similar method for all type-certificated products?

6. The owner of an aircraft with a maximum certificated takeoff weight of 13,000 pounds has been paid for several years by two different companies to fly their executives from place to place. Flights for these two companies are the only flights the aircraft conducts. Under what regulation will the owner's operations be conducted, and why?

7. According to 14 CFR Part 145, who can work at a repair station? What manual is required at a repair station and what does it contain?

8. According to 14 CFR Part 43, what is the difference between a repair and an alteration? Between overhauling and rebuilding? Between major and minor maintenance actions?

<u>Chapter 2</u>

Regulations, Maintenance Forms, Records, and Publications

ANALYSIS
QUESTIONS

name:

date:

Regulations, Maintenance Forms, Records, and Publications

ANALYSIS
QUESTIONS

name:

date:

9. How can you tell whether an Airworthiness Directive applies to a certain aircraft? What must be done if the Airworthiness Directive does, indeed, apply to that aircraft?

10. What are some useful maintenance-related documents not produced by the FAA? What are their limitations?

Mathematics in Aviation Maintenance

FILL IN THE BLANK QUESTIONS

name:

date:

1. The set of numbers that begins 0, 1, 2, 3... is called the set of ________________________.

2. The answer to a subtraction problem is called the ____________________.

3. To add or subtract fractions, the fractions must have the same ____________________.

4. When you divide a/an _____________________ by a divisor, you get a quotient.

5. When the upper and lower numbers in a fraction do not have any _____________________ in common, the fraction is said to be in its lowest terms.

6. The place value of the 7 in 12.075 is _________________________.

7. Rounding 1.736 to the nearest tenth gives you ____________________.

8. To convert a decimal number to the nearest equivalent common fraction, first multiply the decimal number by ___________________. The answer will be the numerator of the fraction, and the number you multiplied by will be the denominator.

9. To convert a fraction to a decimal, divide the ________________________ by the ________________________.

10. These examples—3/5, 3:5, and 3 to 5—are ways to express a/an ____________________.

11. The ____________________ ratio is the inverse or opposite of the speed ratio.

12. To find the missing number in a proportion like 4/25=x/100, you can multiply _____________ by _____________ and then divide by _______________.

13. The product of a positive and _________________________ number is always negative.

14. These numbers—4, 9, 16, 25—are examples of _________________________.

15. This number—1.25×10^3—is written in _________________________.

16. When solving for a/an _________________________ in an equation, you can add, subtract, multiply, and divide the terms in the equation as long as you do the same thing on both sides of the equation.

17. "Please Excuse My Dear Aunt Sally" is a way to remember the _________________________ in algebra. The first letters stand for the first letters of Parentheses, Exponents, Multiplication, Division, Addition, Subtraction.

18. The area of a rectangle 6 inches wide and 4 inches tall is _____________________ inches.

19. The volume of a solid 6 inches wide, 4 inches tall, and 3 inches deep is ________________________ inches.

Mathematics in Aviation Maintenance

FILL IN THE BLANK
QUESTIONS

name:

date:

20. To find the volume of a cylinder, multiply the square of the radius by the height of the cylinder by ________________.

21. The surface area of a solid is measured in ________________ units.

22. The ________________ of an angle is the ratio of the length of the opposite side of the triangle to the length of an adjacent side of the triangle.

23. In the metric system, the prefix "________________" means ten times the base measure.

24. The number 101 in the binary system is the same as ________________ in the decimal system.

1. When adding or subtracting whole numbers:
   a. Align the numbers in columns according to place value.
   b. Align the left side of the numbers.
   c. Always put the smaller number first.
   d. Round off to the nearest ten.

2. Multiplication is the process of repeated:
   a. Subtraction
   b. Addition
   c. Division
   d. None of these

3. The least common denominator for 1/3 and 1/4 is:
   a. 7
   b. 10
   c. 4
   d. 12

4. The sum of 1/3 and 1/4 is:
   a. 2/7
   b. 7/12
   c. 1/12
   d. 3/10

5. In the lowest terms, the product of 8/9 and 9/16 is:
   a. 2/3
   b. 72/144
   c. 1/2
   d. 3/8

6. For a piece of metal 4-1/2" wide by 3-5/8" high, where is the center located?
   a. 2-1/4" from the side, 1-13/16" from the top
   b. 2-1/4" from the side, 1-5/16" from the top
   c. 2-3/8" from the side, 1-1/2" from the top
   d. 2-1/4" from the side, 1-1/2" from the top

7. The number spoken as "one million, thirty thousand and four" is written in numerals as:
   a. 1,300,400
   b. 1,030,040
   c. 1,000,340
   d. 1,030,004

8. What is the total resistance in a series circuit that contains these resistances—0.75, 23.8, and 0.08:
   a. 41.1 ohms
   b. 4.11 ohms
   c. 24.63 ohms
   d. 32.955 ohms

9. What is the wattage of a tool that uses 10.6 amperes from a 120-volt source?
   a. 12,727 watts
   b. 1,272 watts
   c. 127.2 watts
   d. 130.6 watts

10. A series of holes in an aircraft structure must be first drilled to 1/64 undersize and then reamed to the final desired diameter of 0.64. What drill bit should be used for the initial hole?
    a. 41/64"
    b. 5/8"
    c. 3/4"
    d. 21/32"

11. If two gears have a gear ratio of 4:9, the speed ratio of the two gears is:
    a. 4:9
    b. 2:4.5
    c. 9:4
    d. More information is needed to answer this question

12. What is 20 percent of 90?
    a. 180
    b. 18
    c. 2.0
    d. 1.8

MULTIPLE CHOICE
QUESTIONS

name:

date:

13. The expression 4^3 can be read as:
    a. Four to the third power
    b. Four cubed
    c. Four threes
    d. Both A and B

14. The square root of 58 is between:
    a. 3 and 4
    b. 7 and 8
    c. 8 and 9
    d. Can only be estimated with a calculator

15. Convert 3,428,000,000 to scientific notation.
    a. 3.428×10^9
    b. 3.428×10^6
    c. 3.428×10^{-9}
    d. 3.4×10^9

16. Solve this equation: $N = 3 \times [(6-3)^2 \times 4]$
    a. 0
    b. 324
    c. −36
    d. 108

17. Which of these shapes has one set of parallel sides?
    a. Square
    b. Trapezoid
    c. Parallelogram
    d. Triangle

18. The area of the triangle shown in this diagram is:

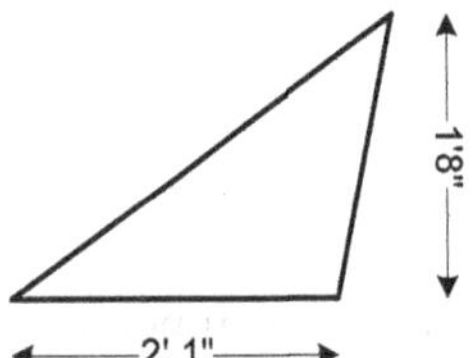

    a. 500 inches
    b. 500 square inches
    c. 250 square inches
    d. 1.89 square feet

19. A circle has a radius of 5 centimeters. What is its circumference?
    a. 31.4 cm^2
    b. 31.4 cm
    c. 25 cm^2
    d. 78.5 cm^2

20. What is the area of the circle in question 19?
    a. 31.4 cm^3
    b. 15.7 cm^3
    c. 25 cm^2
    d. 78.5 cm^2

21. One square meter is equal to:
    a. 1.195 square yards
    b. 2 square yards
    c. 0.384 square yards
    d. 1.95 square yards

22. What is the volume of sphere with a diameter of 5 centimeters?
    a. 522.3 cm^3
    b. 522.3 cm^2
    c. 104.5 cm^3
    d. 78.5 cm^2

23. What is the surface area of the sphere in question 22?
    a. 314.2 cm^3
    b. 104.7 cm^2
    c. 314.2 cm^2
    d. $1,256.6 \text{ cm}^3$

24. Will a square sheet of metal that is 9 feet on each side fit through a cargo door that measures 6 feet by 7 feet?
    a. No.
    b. Yes, with 6 inches to spare.
    c. Yes, with 2 feet to spare.
    d. Yes, with less than 3 inches to spare.

25. The decimal number 137 looks like this in binary numbers:
    a. 11100001
    b. 10001001
    c. 01101101
    d. 10001101

1. What is one way that adding or subtracting decimal numbers is simpler than adding or subtracting fractions?

2. When trying to find the nearest common fraction (like when you're trying to find the right socket size) to a decimal measurement, why does it work to multiply the decimal by 64, round to the nearest whole number, and put the whole number in a fraction over 64?

3. What are three places where ratios are used in aviation? How is each one calculated—what measurement is in relation to what other measurement?

4. A fraction includes a numerator and a denominator separated by a fraction bar. The bar indicates that division is taking place—that is, 3/4 means both "three-fourths" and "three divided by four." What is one way to use this built-in division in calculations?

Chapter 3

Mathematics in Aviation Maintenance

ANALYSIS
QUESTIONS

name:

date:

5. What kinds of numbers are best expressed in scientific notation?

6. Depending on the order of operations in an equation, you can get very different answers. Solve this equation as it is written. Then adding other marks to it—but without changing the numbers or operations themselves—show how you can get three different answers.

   Equation: $6 \times 4 + 3 \times 2 - 1 \times 8 + 2$

7. A rectangle measures 3 inches by 7 inches. What is its area? Now take the same rectangle and imagine it is a box 6 inches deep? What is its volume? And what is the ratio of the area to the volume? Now do the same three calculations with a square and cube measuring 3 inches on each side.

8. What is the circumference of the figure below (to the nearest tenth of an inch)?

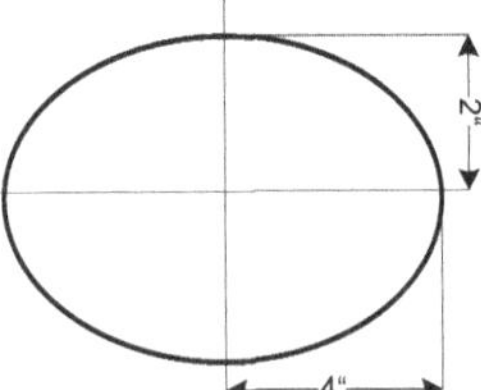

9. How could you check whether a corner is square by using the Pythagorean theorem?

10. What are the benefits of the metric, or International System, versus the conventional U.S. or English system of measurement?

Chapter 3
Mathematics in Aviation Maintenance

ANALYSIS QUESTIONS

name:

date:

1. In reference to aircraft drawings, CAD stands for _______________________.

2. A drawing that shows a single part is called a/an _______________________.

3. A/An _______________________ shows part of an object cut away to reveal interior structures and construction.

4. Information like a drawing number, name of part, scale, and date appears in the _______________________ of an aircraft drawing.

5. The _______________________ lists the materials and parts required for the fabrication or assembly of the component or system shown in a drawing.

6. _______________________ is the allowable variation on a dimension or size. It is usually written with a plus sign (+) and minus sign (–).

7. _______________________ show an object from multiple points of view.

8. A/An _______________________ is a graphic representation of an assembly or system that indicates the various parts and expresses the methods or principles of operation.

9. A/An _______________________ diagram doesn't show the location of parts on an aircraft, but rather shows the relation of parts or their location with respect to each other within a system.

10. A chart that can be used, through answering a series of yes or no questions, to isolate the source of a problem or to suggest a solution to a problem is called a/an _______________________.

11. Distances between holes in an object are usually given from _______________________ to _______________________.

12. Thin lines with alternating long and short dashes indicate the _______________________ of an object.

13. Lines that indicate the relative position of a missing part are called _______________________.

14. There is a whole set of _______________________ used in diagrams to indicate conductors, generators, relays and other elements rather than pictorial views of these elements.

15. One cannot read a drawing by looking at a single view when _______________________ is provided.

16. A/An _______________________ is usually just a simple rough drawing, but it must show enough detail and information for someone else to use it.

FILL IN THE BLANK QUESTIONS

name:

date:

17. Drawing instruments are _____________________ tools that must be properly cared for.

18. The title, notes, and _____________________ on a graph must be read carefully to know what the graph shows.

19. A/An _____________________ is a graph that usually contains three sets of data. Knowing two variables enables you to determine the value for the corresponding third variable.

20. In a digital image, it is important to place a/an _____________________ or some other object of known size next to the area of concern to provide context.

Chapter 4

Aircraft Drawings

MULTIPLE CHOICE
QUESTIONS

name:

date:

1. CADD stands for:
   a. Computer-Aided Design and Drafting
   b. Concept-Added Design and Detail
   c. Computer-Aided Design
   d. Comprehensive Aircraft Design and Drafting

2. CAM stands for:
   a. Comprehensive Aircraft Maintenance
   b. Computer-Aided Maintenance
   c. Computer-Aided Manufacturing
   d. Computer-Assisted Monitoring

3. Drawings and prints are the link between the engineers who design an aircraft and:
   a. The pilots who fly it
   b. The corporations that purchase the aircraft
   c. The workers who build, maintain, and repair the aircraft
   d. None of these

4. A drawing that describes an object made up of two or more parts and shows the relationship between those parts is called a/an:
   a. Detail drawing
   b. Assembly drawing
   c. Installation drawing
   d. Sectional view drawing

5. A drawing that shows a part in its final position in the aircraft is called a/an:
   a. Detail drawing
   b. Assembly drawing
   c. Installation drawing
   d. Sectional view drawing

6. Which of these does not usually appear in the title block of a drawing?
   a. A drawing number
   b. The scale to which the graphic is drawn
   c. The name of the drafting firm
   d. The cost of the assembly

7. The first number in the universal numbering system used to identify drawings:
   a. Consists of six or seven digits
   b. Is always 1, 2, 4, or 5, and indicates the size of the drawing
   c. Is always 3, 4, or 6 and indicates the size of the drawing
   d. Is always 1, 2, 3, 4, or 5, and indicates the scale of the drawing

8. This feature of a drawing is used to locate a particular point on the drawing.
   a. Bill of materials
   b. Revision block
   c. Zone numbers
   d. Notes

9. This feature of a drawing details the changes made to the drawing.
   a. Bill of materials
   b. Revision block
   c. Zone numbers
   d. Notes

10. Station numbers identify:
    a. The distance in inches of a part from a datum, often the nose of the aircraft
    b. The order of assembly
    c. The distance in centimeters of a part from the center of the aircraft
    d. The distance in inches of a part above or below the waterline or buttock line

11. A drawing with a scale of 1:1 shows a part:
    a. At half of its actual size
    b. At its actual size
    c. At twice its actual size, with realistic detail
    d. At its actual size, assuming the printed drawing has not been enlarged or shrunken during the printing process

Chapter 4
Aircraft Drawings

MULTIPLE CHOICE
QUESTIONS

name:

date:

12. A diagram that shows each component of a system and its location in the aircraft is called a/an:
    a. Installation diagram
    b. Schematic diagram
    c. Block diagram
    d. Wiring diagram

13. A diagram that shows a simplified relationship between the components of a complex system without using realistic illustrations is called a/an:
    a. Installation diagram
    b. Schematic diagram
    c. Block diagram
    d. Wiring diagram

14. The line below indicates what?

    a. Center line
    b. A break
    c. A hidden line
    d. Satum line

15. This line is used to show what?

    a. Center line
    b. Phantom line
    c. Dimensions
    d. Visible line

16. This line indicates what?

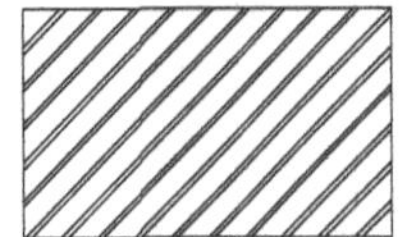

    a. Phantom line
    b. Cutting plane
    c. Visible line
    d. Complex cutting plane

17. This marking in a drawing indicates what type of material?

    a. Cast iron
    b. Steel
    c. Rubber or plastic
    d. Brass or bronze

18. This electrical symbol indicates what?

    a. A condenser
    b. A generator
    c. A circuit breaker
    d. Polarity

19. This electrical symbol indicates what?

    a. A condenser
    b. A generator
    c. A circuit breaker
    d. Polarity

20. A means of storing many drawings, part catalogs, and other information on a card with the pages laid out in grid format is:
    a. Microfilm
    b. Computer disk
    c. Microfiche
    d. Digital images

1. In aircraft maintenance, what are the advantages of drawings over written instructions or the spoken word?

Chapter 4
Aircraft Drawings

2. Why might a drawing not show some parts or portions of some parts? How could this omission make the drawing more clear or useful?

ANALYSIS
QUESTIONS

name:

date:

3. Describe the difference between perspective, isometric, and oblique drawings.

4. Sketch a simple three-dimensional object and then draw six views of it in an orthographic projection in the proper relationship.

5. When would be a good time to use a block diagram rather than an installation or other detailed, realistic type of drawing?

<u>Chapter 5</u>

Physics for Aviation

FILL IN THE BLANK QUESTIONS

name:

date:

1. Whatever occupies space, has mass, and can be perceived by the senses in some way is known as _______________.

2. A/An _______________ is a quantity of mass that will accelerate at a rate of 1 foot per second squared when a force of 1 pound is applied.

3. The _______________ of a substance is its weight per unit of volume.

4. The electrolyte in a discharged battery is 1.15 times denser than _______________.

5. The product of weight and height is known as _______________ energy.

6. The metric unit of measurement for force is the _______________.

7. Force times _______________ equals work.

8. Force times distance divided by _______________ equals power.

9. The length of the crankshaft times the force of pushing down on the piston can be used to calculate the _______________ of an engine.

10. A seesaw is an example of a/an _______________, which is a type of simple machine.

11. A block and tackle is an example of a/an _______________, another type of simple machine.

12. The force that tries to crush an object is called _______________.

13. _______________ is calculated by dividing the change in velocity by the time it took to affect that change.

14. The amount of heat required to change the temperature of 1 gram of water by 1 degree Centigrade is 1 _______________.

15. The process by which heat is transferred by movement of a gas or liquid is called _______________.

16. Pure water boils at 100 degrees on the _______________ scale.

17. The amount of force acting on a specific amount of surface area is known as _______________.

18. If the pressure is held constant, a gas will expand or contract in direct proportion to a change in _______________.

19. The formula, Force = Pressure x Area, is one expression of _______________ law.

Chapter 5

Physics for Aviation

20. Bernoulli's principle concerns the flow of a fluid through a/an _______________ tube.

21. In general, sound travels fastest in solids and slowest in _______________.

22. Standard day atmospheric pressure at sea level is _______________ pounds per square inch.

23. When an aircraft is accelerating, it has more _______________ than drag.

FILL IN THE BLANK QUESTIONS

name:

date:

24. According to Bernoulli's principle, air travelling over the curved upper surface of an aircraft wing must move at a greater velocity than the air travelling under the wing, causing the _______________ on top of the wing to be less than that under the wing, generating lift.

25. A/An _______________ is any device that creates a force when air is made to flow over its surfaces. Examples include an aircraft wing, a propeller blade, and the rotor blade of a helicopter.

26. An airplane that tends to return to its original equilibrium after that equilibrium is disrupted has positive _______________.

27. Movement around the lateral axis of an airplane is called _______________.

28. Movement around the vertical axis of an airplane is controlled by the _______________.

29. _______________ shock waves form at the leading edge and trailing edge of a sharp-edged wing in supersonic flight.

30. The tail rotor on a helicopter counteracts the _______________ produced by the main rotor system.

31. Blade _______________ solves the problem of dissymmetry of lift in helicopters.

32. So-called "trike" aircraft are controlled in flight by pivoting the _______________ forward or aft, and left and right.

33. Powered parachutes climb when the pilot increases or advances the _______________.

Chapter 5

Physics for Aviation

MULTIPLE CHOICE
QUESTIONS

name:

date:

1. Mathematically, weight equals:
    a. Mass divided by acceleration due to gravity
    b. Mass times gravity
    c. Mass plus slug
    d. Mass divided by force

2. A cubic foot of water weighs 62.4 pounds. If a liquid has a specific gravity of 0.75, how much does a cubic foot of that liquid weigh?
    a. 62.4 pounds
    b. 83.2 pounds
    c. 46.8 pounds
    d. 63.15 pounds

3. The potential energy of a 10-pound object suspended 12 feet in the air is:
    a. 120 foot-pounds
    b. 22 foot-pounds
    c. 1.2 foot pounds
    d. Cannot be calculated from this information.

4. A Piper PA-18 Super Cub weighing 1,000 pounds goes down the runway at a velocity of 25 feet per second. How many foot-pounds of kinetic energy does this 1950s-era plane possess?
    a. 25,000 foot-pounds
    b. 12,500 foot-pounds
    c. 625,000 foot-pounds
    d. 312,500 foot-pounds

5. How much work is performed when a 5,000-pound aircraft is jacked up to a vertical height of 5 feet?
    a. 25,000 foot-pounds
    b. 5,005 foot-pounds
    c. 1,000 foot-pounds
    d. 125,000 foot-pounds

6. The force of friction that must be overcome to start an object moving slowly is:
    a. Rolling friction
    b. Sliding friction
    c. Static friction
    d. Science friction

7. How much horsepower is needed to perform the work in question 5 in 3 minutes?
    a. 0.25 hp
    b. 8,333 hp
    c. 0.75 hp
    d. 25,000 hp

8. When calculating torque:
    a. The formula looks the same as the formula for work—that is, force times distance.
    b. Force is applied along a distance and not through a distance.
    c. The units are pound-inches rather than inch-pounds.
    d. All of the above are true.

9. Simple machines can:
    a. Multiply force
    b. Change the direction of force
    c. Both A and B, in addition to other benefits
    d. Make force unnecessary to performing work

10. The effect calculated with the formula Force Out divided by Force Applied is known as:
    a. Torque
    b. Mechanical advantage
    c. Effort
    d. Resistance

11. A lever where the resistance lies between the fulcrum and the effort is called:
    a. First-class lever
    b. Second-class lever
    c. Third-class lever
    d. Fourth-class lever

12. A first-class lever is used to lift a certain object. If the weight is 20 inches from the fulcrum and an effort of 150 pounds applied 40 inches from the fulcrum is required to lift it, how much does the object weigh?
    a. 300 pounds
    b. 30 pounds
    c. 100 pounds
    d. 6,000 pounds

13. The retractable main landing gear on an airplane is an example of what kind of lever?
    a. First-class lever
    b. Second-class lever
    c. Third-class lever
    d. Fourth-class lever

14. The only advantage of a single fixed pulley is:
    a. To magnify the force applied to the weight
    b. To transform the energy applied from mechanical to electrical energy
    c. To increase the speed with which the weight can be moved
    d. To change the direction of the force applied

15. For a machine with gears to magnify the force applied:
    a. A smaller gear must turn a larger gear.
    b. A larger gear must turn a smaller gear.
    c. The gears must be of equal size.
    d. A bevel gear must be used.

16. A loading ramp is an example of what kind of simple machine?
    a. Pulley
    b. Gear
    c. Lever
    d. Inclined plane

17. The stress that an object experiences when it is twisted is known as:
    a. Tension
    b. Compression
    c. Torsion
    d. Shear

18. Speed indicates the rate of motion, but velocity denotes:
    a. The same thing as speed
    b. Both the speed of an object and the direction in which it is moving
    c. Both the direction of an object and its acceleration
    d. Both the acceleration and speed of an object

19. If an airplane increases its velocity by 25 miles per hour in 10 seconds, what is its rate of acceleration in feet per second?
    a. 2.5 fps
    b. 1.70 fps
    c. 3.67 fps
    d. 250 fps

20. Newton's First Law of Motion begins, "Objects at rest tend to remain at rest and objects in motion tend to remain in motion at the same speed and in the same direction," and ends:
    a. "unless acted on by an external force."
    b. "insofar as the future can be predicted."
    c. "until gravity catches up with them."
    d. That's it—the law is complete as stated.

21. A gauge that includes atmospheric pressure in its reading is displaying:
    a. Differential pressure
    b. Gauge pressure
    c. Absolute pressure
    d. Mercurial pressure

22. The pressure on 10 cubic feet of a gas is lessened to the point that the gas expands to 12 cubic feet. The original temperature was 75° F and the original pressure was 800 psig. After the gas expands, the pressure is 820 psig. What is the dangerously high temperature of the expanded gas?
    a. 198° F
    b. 532° Rankine
    c. 658° F
    d. 273° F

23. The floats on a seaplane are required by Title 14 of the *Code of Federal Regulations* part 23 to be 80 percent larger than the minimum needed to support the weight of the plane. If the seaplane weighs 15,000 lbs., what is the required volume of the floats?
    a. 240 ft^3
    b. 433 ft^3
    c. 867 ft^3
    d. 192 ft^3

24. In a two-piston hydraulic system, the input piston has an area of 0.4 in^2 and the output piston has an area of 12 in^2. An input force of 46 lbs. is applied and the input piston moves 25 inches. What is the mechanical advantage?
    a. 1380 lb.
    b. 16
    c. 115 psi
    d. 12

25. In the scenario in question 24, how far does the output piston move?
    a. 8 inches
    b. 0.83 inches
    c. 0.76 inches
    d. 9.58 inches

26. A Mach number describes the ratio of the speed of an aircraft to:
    a. The decibels created by the aircraft's engines
    b. The ambient air pressure
    c. The speed of sound
    d. The pitch of the aircraft's wings

27. The composition of the air remains almost constant from sea level up to the highest altitude, but:
    a. Its density diminishes rapidly
    b. Its temperature increases to a height of seven miles
    c. Its pressure increases rapidly
    d. Its pressure increases and decreases passing through the various atmospheric bands

28. The layer of the atmosphere that extends from the earth's surface to about 35,000 feet at middle latitudes is called the:
    a. Troposphere
    b. Ionosphere
    c. Mesosphere
    d. Exosphere

29. The boundary layer of air that flows smoothly over a wing is called:
    a. The turbulent layer
    b. The laminar layer
    c. The transition layer
    d. The vortex

30. The most common lift-modifying device—flaps—change the camber of a wing and act to:
    a. Decrease the lift and increase the drag at steeper angles of attack
    b. Increase the lift and decrease the drag at low speeds
    c. Increase both the lift and the drag at flatter angles of attack
    d. Increase both the lift and the drag at any angle of attack

31. The difference between the speed of sound at sea level and the speed of sound at 25,000 feet is:
    a. 692 mph
    b. 761 mph
    c. 69 mph
    d. 54 mph

MULTIPLE CHOICE QUESTIONS

name:

date:

MULTIPLE CHOICE
QUESTIONS

name:

date:

32. The cyclic pitch control lever in a helicopter controls:
    a. The pitch of the blades, allowing the helicopter to move left, right, forward, or backward
    b. The speed of the blades
    c. The pitch of the blades, allowing the helicopter to rise vertically
    d. The anti-torque rotor, keeping the helicopter stable

33. Autorotation is a flight condition where:
    a. The main rotor blades move because of inertia.
    b. The main rotor blade reverses direction to lower the helicopter.
    c. The main rotor blades are driven by the force of the relative wind passing through them rather than by the engine.
    d. The engine is using fuel at its maximum recommended rate.

1. Describe the two main types of energy and how each can be converted to the other type.

2. What is the difference between work and a kind of force called torque? Describe how force and torque work in a piston engine.

3. Force creates stress. Describe three types of stress and give examples of aircraft parts or systems subject to each one.

<u>Chapter 5</u>

Physics for Aviation

ANALYSIS
QUESTIONS

name:

date:

4. Give examples to demonstrate each of Newton's three laws of motion.

5. Describe three ways in which heat is transferred from one location to another.

6. Describe the difference between gauge pressure, absolute pressure, and differential pressure readings.

7. What are the effects of humid air on aircraft performance?

8. Bernoulli's principle and Newton's third law are two ways of looking at the same phenomena. Explain how each of these laws of physics explains the lift on a wing.

9. Why is boundary layer flow important? How do aircraft mechanics and designers attempt to control boundary layer flow?

10. Name and define the three axes of an airplane. Then name the type of movement around each axis, list the airplane controls that move the craft around each axis, and give the equivalent helicopter controls.

Chapter 5
Physics for Aviation

ANALYSIS
QUESTIONS

name:

date:

Chapter 6

Aircraft Weight and Balance

FILL IN THE BLANK
QUESTIONS

name:

date:

1. The maximum weight of an aircraft is based on the amount of lift the _________________ can provide under the operating conditions for which the aircraft is designed.

2. Over time, almost all aircraft tend to gain _________________.

3. The _________________ is an imaginary vertical plane from which all horizontal measurements are taken for balance purposes.

4. Important weight and balance information for an aircraft certificated after 1958 can be found on the _________________.

5. The _________________ is the horizontal distance from the datum to any point in the aircraft.

6. A/An _________________ is measured in inch-pounds and represents the torque value of a part of the aircraft.

7. Weight being added to an aircraft aft of the datum produces a/an _________________ moment.

8. The heaviest allowable weight to which an aircraft can be loaded without usable fuel in its tanks is called the _________________.

9. If you subtract the empty weight of an aircraft from its maximum allowable weight, you get the _________________.

10. For piston engine–powered aircraft, _________________ is calculated as one-half pound of fuel for each METO (maximum except takeoff) horsepower of the engine.

11. An aircraft must be in level _________________ when it is weighed.

12. The weight of aircraft fuel can be measured with a/an _________________.

13. Never weigh an aircraft with the fuel tanks _________________, as it will be impossible to figure out exactly how much fuel to account for.

14. The arm for each weighing point is the distance from the center of the _________________ to the datum.

15. The standard weight for lubricating oil is _________________ pounds per gallon.

16. The center of gravity is calculated by dividing the _________________ by the total weight of the aircraft.

17. In a/an _________________, all useful load items in front of the forward CG limit are loaded and all useful load items behind the forward CG limit are left empty.

FILL IN THE BLANK
QUESTIONS

name:

date:

18. After new aircraft equipment is installed, mathematical calculation of the new weight and balance is acceptable if the exact _________________________and _________________________ of all the changes are known.

19. _________________________ should always be placed as far away from the affected limit as possible.

20. According to Figure 6-44, if the aircraft had a load weight of 2,200 lbs. and a loaded moment of 85,000 in.-lbs., the weight and balance would be within the _________________________.

21. Helicopters have a longitudinal center of gravity, like airplanes, but also have _________________________ center of gravity.

22. Before weighing a helicopter, it is usually leveled using a/an _________________________.

23. The most significant factor affecting the weight and balance of a single-seat "trike" aircraft is the weight of the _________________________.

24. The average width of a tapered, swept-back wing is known as the _________________________.

25. When a technician is involved with the weight and balance of an aircraft, it almost always involves a calculation of the aircraft's empty _________________________ and empty _________________________: only rarely does it involve calculating ballast or extreme conditions.

1. A weight and balance report includes which of the following items?
   a. The empty weight of the aircraft
   b. Average fuel consumption at standard air speed
   c. The location of the aircraft's center of gravity
   d. Both A and C

2. An item forward of the datum has:
   a. A negative arm
   b. A restricted arm
   c. A positive arm
   d. Unlimited arm

3. The moment of a 12-pound box located 30 inches aft of the datum is:
   a. 36 inch-pounds
   b. –36 inch-pounds
   c. 360 inch-pounds
   d. –360 inch-pounds

4. The moment of a 5-pound control lever located 5 inches forward of the datum is:
   a. 55 inch-pounds
   b. –55 inch-pounds
   c. 25 inch-pounds
   d. –25 inch-pounds

5. Which of the following items are not included in an aircraft's empty weight?
   a. Hydraulic fluid
   b. Residual fuel and oil
   c. Powerplant
   d. All the above are included in the empty weight

6. If the maximum allowable gross weight of an airplane is 2,000 pounds and the empty weight is 950 pounds, what is the useful load?
   a. 950 pounds
   b. 1,050 pounds
   c. 2,000 pounds
   d. 2,950 pounds

7. The weight of equipment used to support a plane during weighing, including wheel chocks and ground locks, is called:
   a. Tare weight
   b. Minimum weight
   c. Usable load
   d. Ramp weight

8. Where is the center of gravity if the total moment is 47,000 inch-pounds and the total weight is 625 pounds?
   a. 75.2 pounds
   b. 75.2 inches
   c. 47 inch-pounds
   d. 75.3 inches

9. Where is the center of gravity if the total weight is 500 pounds and the total moment is 4,500 inch-pounds?
   a. 0.1 inches
   b. 9 pounds
   c. 9 inches
   d. 9.1 inches

10. What item placed on top of a jack can be used to weigh an aircraft?
    a. A load cell
    b. Mechanical balance
    c. Sliding weight pack
    d. Platform-type electronic scale

11. To help measure the distance from an aircraft's datum to part of the aircraft, which of the following tools is most useful?
    a. Spirit level
    b. Plumb bob
    c. Hydrometer
    d. Load cell

Chapter 6

Aircraft Weight and Balance

MULTIPLE CHOICE
QUESTIONS

name:

date:

<u>Chapter 6</u>

Aircraft Weight and Balance

MULTIPLE CHOICE
QUESTIONS

name:

date:

12. To ensure that an aircraft's weight includes only residual fuel weight, which of these methods is recommended?
    a. Weigh the aircraft with absolutely no fuel in the tanks or lines, then add the proper amount of residual fuel to the total
    b. Weigh the aircraft with only residual fuel weight in the tanks
    c. Weigh the aircraft completely full of fuel, subtract the weight of usable fuel, and account for its arm and moment
    d. Any of these

13. According to the Type Certificate Data Sheet information shown in Figure 6-24, what is the center of gravity range for the Piper Seneca, serial number 34-7250135, at 3,400 pounds?
    a. +86.4 to +94.6
    b. +87.9 to +94.6
    c. +82.0 to +94.6
    d. +80.7 to +94.6

14. Unless the actual weight is known, the standard weight of an aircraft crew member, for the purposes of weight and balance, is:
    a. 150 pounds
    b. 180 pounds
    c. 175 pounds
    d. 170 pounds

15. According to the Center of Gravity Envelope shown in Figure 6-25, what is the maximum landing weight for the Piper Seneca?
    a. 4,000 pounds
    b. 2,780 pounds
    c. 3,200 pounds
    d. None of these

16. According to the data shown in Figure 6-27, how is the tricycle gear airplane used in the example leveled?
    a. By placing a level on the horizontal stabilizer.
    b. Using two screws on the left side of the fuselage below the window
    c. By fully inflating the tires
    d. By setting the rudder to a neutral position

17. According to the Type Certificate Data Sheet shown in Figure 6-33, what is the location of the three middle-row seats on the Piper Seneca?
    a. +85.5
    b. +112.5
    c. +155.7
    d. +118.1

18. Weight bolted to the aircraft structure to compensate for the removal or installation of equipment is called:
    a. Ballast
    b. Permanent ballast
    c. Compensatory weighting
    d. Temporary ballast

19. The loaded weight of an aircraft is 3,500 pounds and the center of gravity is 0.75 inches too far aft. How much ballast should be installed 50 inches aft of the aft center of gravity limit?
    a. 52.5 pounds
    b. 50 pounds
    c. 53 pounds
    d. 172.8 pounds

20. According to the graph in Figure 6-43, what is the moment of a 180-pound pilot?
    a. 6
    b. 6,000
    c. 4
    d. 7

21. According to the specifications for a Bell JetRanger helicopter (page 6-29), what are the lateral center of gravity limits when the longitudinal center of gravity is 106 inches?
    a. 2.3 inches left to 4.0 inches right
    b. 3.0 inches left o 4.0 inches right
    c. 2.3 inches left to 3.7 inches right
    d. 2.3 inches left to 3.0 inches right

22. If the pilot of a powered parachute is very heavy, what is adjusted to compensate?
    a. The wing attach point is moved forward
    b. The wing attach point is moved aft
    c. The pivot bar is moved forward
    d. The pivot bar is moved aft

23. What is unusual about weighing a Boeing 747-400 or a Boeing 777?
    a. Many technicians are required to balance such a large aircraft.
    b. Weighing is not required on such a large aircraft.
    c. The axles contain load cells and the plane can essentially weigh itself.
    d. The mean aerodynamic chord is 62 inches.

24. If the center of gravity on a large aircraft is identified as 25 percent of the MAC and the MAC is 104 inches, and the leading edge of the MAC has an arm of 850 inches, where does the center of gravity fall?
    a. 26 inches
    b. 876 inches
    c. 954 inches
    d. 824 inches

<u>Chapter 6</u>

Aircraft Weight and Balance

MULTIPLE CHOICE QUESTIONS

name:

date:

1. What are the two primary reasons that an aircraft mechanic should be concerned with aircraft weight and balance?

2. Find the arm of the center of gravity for the weights as shown in this diagram.

50 lb.	70 lb.	120 lb.		50 lb.	24 lb.	20 lb.	110 lb.
10"	55"	75"		120"	130"	160"	185"

3. Assume you have placed a three-wheeled aircraft on three scales and leveled it. The datum is at the leading edge of the wing. The two rear wheels are at +60", and the front wheel is at –20". Each wheel required two 4-pound chocks. The fuel tanks are full (35 gallons at +90") and there is 6 lb. of unusable fuel at +94". The oil is full.

The nose wheel scale registers 250 lb. The left rear wheel scale shows 680 lb., and the right rear wheel shows 660 lb. What is the arm of the center of gravity?

Chapter 6
Aircraft Weight and Balance

ANALYSIS
QUESTIONS

name:

date:

ANALYSIS
QUESTIONS

name:

date:

4. Take the plane in Question 4 and add the following load items and considerations to it for a flight:

   • 1 pilot, 175 pounds at 25"
   • 1 passenger, 190 pounds at 70"
   • Baggage, 75 pounds at 70"
   • Crate of rocks, 120 pounds at 90"
   • Remember to include a full tank of fuel this time
   • Throw out whatever decimal places you found for the empty center of gravity and use the nearest whole number—this will slightly affect the empty weight moment.

   What is the new center of gravity? Do you think the plane is safe to fly? How could you know for sure?

5. What documents can provide weight and balance information for an aircraft?

<u>Chapter 7</u>

Aircraft Materials, Hardware, and Processes

FILL IN THE BLANK QUESTIONS

name:

date:

1. A metal that can be hammered, rolled, or pressed into various shapes without cracking, breaking, or otherwise being damaged is said to be ________________.

2. ________________ is the ability of metal to resist deformation.

3. ________________ is the property that enables a metal to return to its original size and shape when a force that caused a change of shape is removed.

4. The ability of a metal to become liquid when heated is called ________________.

5. The property that enables a metal to carry heat or electricity is ________________.

6. Metals in which ________________ is the principal component are called ferrous metals.

7. Low-carbon steel contains carbon in percentages from 0.10 to ________________.

8. ________________ is a nickel-chromium-iron alloy that resembles stainless steel in appearance, but is much easier to weld.

9. Aluminum, titanium, copper, and magnesium are all examples of ________________ metals used in aircraft construction.

10. ________________ alloys of aluminum are more widely used in aircraft construction than casting alloys.

11. ________________ is about 60 percent heavier than aluminum, but 50 percent lighter than stainless steel.

12. The ________________ strength of a material is its resistance to a force that tends to pull it apart.

13. The ________________ strength of a material is its resistance to twisting.

14. Usually, the more malleable and ________________ a metal is, the more cold working it can stand.

15. Any process that involves controlled heating and cooling of metals to develop desirable characteristics like hardness, softness, or ductility is called ________________.

16. The usual method for accurately measuring temperature in a furnace is through a/an ________________.

17. After metal has been heated, it is kept at that high temperature for a period of time. Keeping the metal at that temperature is known as ________________.

18. Cooling a metal in the air, in water, or in another medium is called ________________.

FILL IN THE BLANK
QUESTIONS

name:

date:

19. The opposite of hardening steel is _______________________.

20. A/An _______________________ measures the hardness of steel by measuring the depth of the impression left by penetrator.

21. The process by which a metal rod is reduced in diameter by pulling it through increasingly narrow dies is an example of _______________________.

22. _______________________ materials will soften when heated and harden when cooled.

23. Parts that prevent fluid from passing a certain point and also keep air and dirt out of a system are generally called _______________________.

24. Butyl, Buna-S, and neoprene are types of synthetic _______________________.

25. A one-inch diameter National Fine bolt has 14 threads per inch, but a one-inch diameter Unified Fine bolt has _______________________ threads per inch.

26. AN310 specifies a/an _______________________ nut.

27. Using a plain washer under a/an _______________________ prevents damage to the surface material.

28. An aircraft rivet has a formed head on one end of the shank, and another "_______________________" at the other end when properly installed.

29. The material used in for the majority of aircraft solid-shank rivets is _______________________ alloy.

30. _______________________ are the most commonly used threaded fastening devices on an aircraft.

31. A 7 x 19 cable is made up of seven strands of _______________________ wires each.

32. A/An _______________________ is a mechanical screw device consisting of two threaded terminals and a threaded barrel, and it is used to make minor adjustments to cable tension and length.

33. _______________________ is a method of wiring together two or more units in such a manner that any tendency of one to loosen is counteracted by the tightening of the wire.

1. A steel alloy with 1.75% manganese is designated with the series number:
   a. 100xx
   b. 13xx
   c. 41xx
   d. 52xxx

2. In a spark test, nickel steel produces:
   a. Long shafts that are straw colored as they leave the stone but white at the end
   b. Long, straight shafts with a few white sprigs
   c. Small white blocks of light within the main burst
   d. Sparks that are red as they leave the stone and then turn straw colored

3. Steel with a carbon content of 1 percent is classified as:
   a. High-carbon steel
   b. Medium-carbon steel
   c. Low-carbon steel
   d. Nickel-carbon steel

4. Wrought aluminum alloyed with silicon is designed by what series of numbers?
   a. 2xxx
   b. 3xxx
   c. 4xxx
   d. 6xxx

5. The world's lightest structural metal, whose alloys are used in some aircraft nosewheel doors, aileron cover skin, oil tanks, and elsewhere, is:
   a. Magnesium
   b. Aluminum
   c. Titanium
   d. Iron

6. A titanium base alloy that is used for primary structural members, has a yield strength of 110,000 psi, and contains 8 percent manganese, is designated with the code:
   a. A-55
   b. C-110M
   c. A-110AT
   d. A-70

7. A hot-working process that relieves internal stresses, softens the metal, makes it more ductile, and refines the grain structure is:
   a. Normalizing
   b. Extruding
   c. Tempering
   d. Annealing

8. Most nonferrous metals can be:
   a. Casehardened
   b. Tempered
   c. Normalized
   d. None of these

9. Steel alloyed with 1.8 percent nickel and 0.25 percent molybdenum should be quenched in:
   a. Water
   b. Brine
   c. Oil
   d. The air

10. When steel is heated, the particles of iron carbide are dissolved into a solid solution called:
    a. Austenite
    b. Ferrite
    c. Moltenite
    d. Inconel

11. When hardening carbon steel, the metal must be cooled—in less than 1 second—to a temperature below:
    a. 2,000° F
    b. 2,500° F
    c. 1,000° F
    d. 1,750° F

12. Carburizing, cyaniding, and nitriding are common forms of:
    a. Food poisoning
    b. Casehardening
    c. Annealing
    d. Tempering

13. Which of the following techniques can increase the strength of aluminum?
    a. Alloying
    b. Cold working
    c. Heat treatment
    d. All the above

Chapter 7

Aircraft Materials, Hardware, and Processes

MULTIPLE CHOICE QUESTIONS

name:

date:

MULTIPLE CHOICE
QUESTIONS

name:

date:

14. What aluminum alloy type rivet listed below is too hard for driving and must be reheat treated before they can be used?
 a. Alloy 1100
 b. Alloy 5056
 c. Alloy 2017
 d. Alloy 2117

15. When heat treating magnesium alloys, which of these should you _never_ do?
 a. Perform solution heat treatment
 b. Use aging or precipitation heat treatment
 c. Soak the metal in a salt bath
 d. Air quenching

16. A portable hardness tester used to test relatively soft materials in small spaces is:
 a. The Barcol tester
 b. The Rockwell tester
 c. The Brinell tester
 d. The Dia-Matic tester

17. The process of melting metal and pouring it into a mold of the desired shape is:
 a. Forging
 b. Cold working
 c. Casting
 d. Extruding

18. The process of forming metal by hammering or pressing is called:
 a. Forging
 b. Cold working
 c. Casting
 d. Extruding

19. Repeated cold working of metal:
 a. Increases its ductility
 b. Increases its strength and hardness
 c. Makes the metal less brittle
 d. Increases fusibility

20. Which of the following is not an advantage of composite materials?
 a. High strength-to-weight ratio
 b. Longer life than metals
 c. Cost
 d. Tensile strength four to six times that of steel or aluminum

21. A composite with an inner core of material made of rigid foam, wood, metal, or a honeycomb design is called a/an:
 a. Sandwich laminate
 b. Reinforced laminate
 c. Solid laminate
 d. Whisker or fiber

22. The synthetic rubber often used for oil and gasoline hoses, tank linings, gaskets, and seals is:
 a. Butyl
 b. Buna-S
 c. Buna-N
 d. Neoprene

23. What type of seal is generally used in units that contain moving parts?
 a. Packings
 b. Gaskets
 c. Wipers
 d. One-part sealants

24. The type of seal used between two flat surfaces is:
 a. Packings
 b. Gaskets
 c. Wipers
 d. One-part sealants

25. The general purpose hex head aircraft bolt (AN-3 through AN-20) can be used in applications where:
 a. The bolt will only move into position when struck with a 12- to 14-ounce hammer
 b. There is a clearance of 0.006 inches in a 5/8-inch hole, and other size holes in proportion
 c. A right-hand thread is mandatory
 d. The fit is described as Class 4

26. AN standard steel bolt heads are marked with:
    a. A raised dash or asterisk
    b. Two raised dashes
    c. A raised dot
    d. A countersunk head

27. A special-purpose bolt used to permanently attach two materials is the:
    a. Clevis bolt
    b. Eyebolt
    c. Hex bolt
    d. Lockbolt

28. Which of the following non-self-locking nuts is used where the desired tightness can be obtained with the fingers and where the assembly is frequently removed?
    a. AN320
    b. AN350
    c. AN316
    d. AN340

29. When using a steel bolt to secure aluminum alloy or magnesium alloy members, use:
    a. A steel washer under the head of the bolt and the nut
    b. A steel washer under the bolt only
    c. An aluminum alloy washer under the head of the bolt and the nut
    d. A plastic or rubber washer

30. "Icebox" rivets attain their full strength:
    a. 1 hour after driving
    b. 15 minutes after they are removed from cold storage
    c. Four weeks after annealing
    d. About four days after driving

31. The manufactured head of a carbon steel rivet is marked with:
    a. A raised cross
    b. A recessed triangle
    c. A raised dot
    d. Recessed double dots

32. Rivets seldom, if ever, used on an aircraft's exterior skin are:
    a. Flathead
    b. Roundhead
    c. Brazier head
    d. Countersunk head

33. A machine screw designated as AN515 is:
    a. A fillister head screw
    b. A countersunk screw
    c. A roundhead screw
    d. A self-tapping screw

Chapter 7
Aircraft Materials, Hardware, and Processes

MULTIPLE CHOICE QUESTIONS

name:

date:

1. When choosing a type of metal for an aircaft part, what considerations are made regarding its characteristics and th part's application?

2. Name three metals with which steel is commonly alloyed and state the alloy's effect on the steel.

3. What characteristics of aluminum make it so widely used in aircraft construction?

Chapter 7
Aircraft Materials, Hardware, and Processes

ANALYSIS
QUESTIONS

name:

date:

4. Compare the properties of magnesium and titanium and describe their uses in aircraft construction.

5. Describe the equipment used in heat treating.

6. Describe the annealing process for steel and the same process for aluminum alloys. How are they different? What is the purpose of annealing?

7. Threaded fasteners are usually identified by one of three sets of numbers. What are the numbering systems and what do they mean? What effect do the numbering systems have on aircraft repair practices?

ANALYSIS QUESTIONS

name:

8. What are the three main types of torque wrenches, and how is each one used? Why is torque important when installing nuts, bolts, studs, or screws?

date:

9. How do self-plugging rivets—also known as friction-lock rivets—work?

10. What is the point of safety wiring, and what are some general rules for its practice?

1. In-depth information on corrosion control is available in FAA Advisory Circular (AC) ___________________________, Corrosion Control for Aircraft.

2. Metal corrosion is the deterioration of the metal by chemical or ___________________________ attack.

3. The speed of electrochemical attack is increased in a hot, ___________________ climate.

4. Pure ___________________________ corrosion results from direct exposure of bare metal to caustic liquid or gaseous agents.

5. ___________________________ corrosion can be the result of the lack of uniformity in the alloy structure.

6. ___________________________ deposits are very corrosive and can cause problems where gaps, seams, hinges, and fairings are downstream from exhaust pipes or nozzles.

7. The ___________________________ area receives more punishment due to mud, water, salt, gravel, and other flying debris than any other area on the aircraft, and thus may be particularly prone to corrosion problems.

8. The first step in removing corrosion is to remove ___________________________ covering the attacked or suspected area.

9. The presence of ___________________________ on ferrous metals actually promotes additional corrosion because it attracts moisture from the air and acts as a catalyst for further damage.

10. Because pure ___________________________ has more corrosion resistance than its stronger alloys, a thin coating of it is often applied over the base alloy.

11. ___________________________ is the most chemically active metal used in aircraft construction and thus is the most difficult to protect from corrosion.

12. Certain metals in contact with other metals are subject to ___________________________ or dissimilar metals corrosion.

13. The descriptive classification for the worst corrosion damage is "damage ___________________________."

14. Chemical cleaning of surfaces is preferred to ___________________________ because none of the base metal is removed by the cleaning.

15. The most common surface chemical treatment for nonclad aluminum alloys is ___________________________.

FILL IN THE BLANK
QUESTIONS

name:

date:

16. Plastic surfaces should be washed with _________________________, preferably by hand.

17. Because aircraft cabins are small, restricted enclosures, _________________ cleaning agents should be used whenever possible to reduce fire and explosion hazards.

18. The most common petroleum-based dry cleaning solvent used in aircraft cleaning is _________________ solvent, which has a flashpoint slightly above 105° F.

19. MIL-C-5410 Type I and _________________ materials are safe to use on all painted and unpainted surfaces, as well as fabrics, leather, and transparent plastics.

20. _________________ may be used to neutralize acid deposits in lead-acid battery compartments.

1. Aircraft with airframes built primarily of composite components are still subject to corrosion because:
   a. Composites can, under some circumstances, corrode.
   b. Composites do not have the protection against corrosion that some metal parts have.
   c. Metal components and accessories are still used within the airframe.
   d. Salt water is attracted to composite material.

2. The surface of corroding aluminum alloys or magnesium:
   a. Has pitting or etching, often with gray or white powdery deposits
   b. Has reddish rust
   c. Has a greenish film
   d. Is unmarked, as these metals corrode from the inside out

3. The surface of corroding copper or copper alloys:
   a. Has pitting or etching, often with gray or white powdery deposits
   b. Has reddish rust
   c. Has a greenish film
   d. Is unmarked, as these metals corrode from the inside out

4. In all types of corrosion, the metal is converted into:
   a. A gas
   b. A metallic compound, such as an oxide, hydroxide, or sulfate
   c. A liquid
   d. An electrochemical

5. Which of the following is not a common cause of direct chemical attack corrosion?
   a. Spilled battery acid or fumes from batteries
   b. Anodizing
   c. Residual flux from inadequately cleaned, welded, brazed, or soldered joints
   d. Trapped caustic cleaning solutions

6. Electrochemical corrosion requires:
   a. A conductive fluid and metals with a difference in electrical potential
   b. An aluminum alloy and a conductive fluid
   c. Hydrogen gas and salt
   d. Intergranular metals placed next to copper

7. A metal is more likely to corrode with electrochemical processes if it has less:
   a. Malleability
   b. Ductility
   c. Nobility
   d. Hardness

8. Corrosion that looks like a series of small worms under the paint surface is called:
   a. Fretting corrosion
   b. Dissimilar metal corrosion
   c. Intergranular corrosion
   d. Filiform corrosion

9. When two mating surfaces, normally at rest in relation to one another, are subject to slight relative motion, corrosion may appear as pitting of the surfaces and considerable quantities of fine, trapped debris. This is called:
   a. Fretting corrosion
   b. Dissimilar metal corrosion
   c. Intergranular corrosion
   d. Filiform corrosion

10. An external part of the aircraft that is especially prone to corrosion because of the contact of different metals and the way this part tends to trap dirt and moisture is:
    a. Piano-type hinges
    b. Cooling air vents
    c. Bilge areas
    d. Wheel well

Chapter 8

Cleaning and Corrosion Control

MULTIPLE CHOICE
QUESTIONS

name:

date:

11. The most practical means of controlling the corrosion of steel is:
    a. Light brushing with nonmetallic scrapers and restoration of preventive coating
    b. Completely removing corrosion products mechanically and restoring the preventive coating
    c. Polishing and waxing
    d. Scrubbing with nonwoven abrasive pads and re-anodizing the surface

12. Aluminum and aluminum alloys:
    a. Commonly form a thin, smooth surface oxidation that is not considered detrimental, but rather provides a hard barrier to the introduction of corrosive elements.
    b. Are often clad with a relatively pure aluminum coating that offers excellent corrosion resistance
    c. Can withstand considerable corrosive attack before serious loss of structural strength occurs
    d. All the above

13. Corrosive attacks on this metal are probably the easiest type to see because the corrosion products occupy several times the volume of the original metal destroyed and quickly develop into snow-like mounds.
    a. Aluminum
    b. Magnesium
    c. Steel
    d. Titanium

14. Joints involving contact between different types of metal, neither of which is magnesium, are treated with:
    a. At least two coats of zinc chromate or epoxy primer in addition to normal primer requirements
    b. One layer of pressure-sensitive tape in addition to normal primer requirements
    c. A solution of sodium dichromate or epoxy primer in addition to normal primer requirements
    d. Muriatic acid in addition to normal primer requirements

15. If you find corrosion classified as "negligible," you should:
    a. Alert the aircraft owner
    b. Ignore the problem, which is clearly minor
    c. Clean, treat, and paint the metal as appropriate
    d. Replace the affected metal section

16. Parts made of this metal can be pickled in muriatic or sulfuric acid to remove rust, scale, and other foreign matter.
    a. Aluminum
    b. Magnesium
    c. Steel
    d. Lead

17. While anodizing can only be used on nonclad aluminum alloy surfaces, this treatment can be used on all aluminum alloys.
    a. Alodizing
    b. Pickling
    c. Zinc plating
    d. Carbon tetrachloride

18. Aircraft cleaning can be accomplished through:
    a. Dry washing
    b. Polishing
    c. Wet washing
    d. Any of these

19. The recommended solution for wiping down cleaned surfaces just before painting, which can also be used to clean acrylics and rubber, is:
    a. Aromatic naphtha
    b. Aliphatic naphtha
    c. Carbon tetrachloride
    d. Kerosene

20. Which of the following mechanical cleaning materials should not be used on aircraft metals, especially aluminum or magnesium?
    a. Scotch-Brite
    b. Powdered pumice
    c. Carborundum (silicon carbide) paper
    d. Aluminum oxide paper

1. Describe the difference between direct chemical attack and electrochemical attack. How are the results of each process similar?

Chapter 8
Cleaning and Corrosion Control

ANALYSIS
QUESTIONS

name:

date:

2. What factors affect corrosion?

3. Give an overview of the maintenance methods used to prevent corrosion.

<u>Chapter 8</u>

Cleaning and Corrosion Control

ANALYSIS
QUESTIONS

name:

date:

4. How is corrosion treated and corrected on ferrous metals?

5. Why is interior cleaning of an aircraft important for corrosion control? What areas of the aircraft interior require the most attention?

<u>Chapter 9</u>
Fluid Lines and Fittings

FILL IN THE BLANK
QUESTIONS

name:

date:

1. The fluid lines in hydraulic systems with pressures of 3,000 psi or more are made of corrosion-resistant, annealed _______________________.

2. A small rigid tube with _______________________ bands painted on it is made of aluminum alloy number 5052.

3. Metal tubing is sized by its _______________________ diameter.

4. Metal tubing is usually cut with a tube cutting tool, but it can also be cut with a fine-toothed _______________________.

5. Metal tubes with an outside diameter of 1/4" or less are usually bent _______________________, without the use of a bending tool.

6. A flaring tool acceptable for use on aircraft tubing produces flares of _______________________degrees.

7. A double flare is used on soft aluminum alloy tubing with an outside diameter of _______________________ or less.

8. Tapes and decals that identify what a fluid line carries are generally placed at both ends of the line and at least one in each _______________________.

9. _______________________ fittings, which require a bead and a hose and hose clamps, are used only on low- or medium-pressure tubing, such as those found in vacuum or coolant systems.

10. The number following the AN number for a fitting indicates the size of tubing or hose for which the fitting is made in _______________________ of an inch.

11. MS _______________________ fitting are designed primarily for high-pressure (3,000 psi) hydraulic systems that could be subjected to severe vibration or fluctuating pressure.

12. _______________________ fittings contract to their original size shortly after being removed from liquid nitrogen, biting down on a tube and forming a permanent seal.

13. When installing a flareless tube, tighten the nut with your fingers or a wrench to the point where the nut begins to bottom. Then turn the nut an additional _______________________ turn.

14. Scratches or nicks not deeper than _______________________ of the wall thickness in aluminum alloy tubing, which are not in the heel of a bend, may be repaired by burnishing with hand tools.

Chapter 9
Fluid Lines and Fittings

15. If you remove a damaged section of tubing and the distance between the ends is less than _____________________, you can swage a tube-to-tube union in the gap to repair the tubing without replacing the tubing.

16. Low-pressure rubber flexible hoses can handle pressure below _____________________.

17. Tetrafluoroethylene resin, used to manufacture some flexible hose, is better known by its trade name: _____________________.

18. Flexible hose _____________________ in length and expands in diameter when pressure is applied, so 5 to 8 percent of the hose's total length must be provided in slack.

19. You can tell whether a flexible hose is twisted by looking at the _____________________ running along its length.

20. A/An _____________________ clamp is used to secure lines subject to vibration.

1. Rigid metal tubing is used:
   a. In stationary applications
   b. For fuel, oil, coolant, oxygen, and hydraulic lines
   c. In locations subject to considerable vibration
   d. Both A and B

2. Flexible hose is used:
   a. In stationary applications
   b. For fuel, oil, coolant, oxygen, and hydraulic lines
   c. In locations subject to considerable vibration
   d. Both B and C

MULTIPLE CHOICE
QUESTIONS

3. Which of these aluminum alloy tubing is likely to be used in low-pressure instrument lines and ventilating conduits?
   a. CRES 304
   b. 2024-T3
   c. 1100 H14 (1/2 hard)
   d. 5052-O

name:

4. In areas where there is a risk of foreign object damage, what type of metal tubing is most often used?
   a. Aluminum alloy
   b. Steel
   c. Copper
   d. Titanium

date:

5. Aluminum alloy 3003 tubing is marked with:
   a. A white band
   b. A label with a pattern of circles
   c. A red band
   d. A green band

6. Number 10 metal tubing has an outside diameter of:
   a. 5/8"
   b. 9/16"
   c. 1/4"
   d. 3/8"

7. The inside diameter of number 8 metal tubing with a wall thickness of 0.05" is:
   a. 0.50"
   b. 0.45"
   c. 0.40"
   d. 0.55"

8. What is the standard bend radius for number 18 metal tubing?
   a. 2"
   b. 1 1/4"
   c. 3 1/2"
   d. 3"

9. A flareless fitting does not require tube flaring but requires another operation known as:
   a. Beading
   b. Presetting
   c. Rolling
   d. Annealing

10. Lines that contain physically dangerous materials, like oxygen, nitrogen, or Freon, may be labeled:
    a. FLAM
    b. TOXIC
    c. PHDAN
    d. CAUT

11. Do not lubricate the fitting threads in this type of line:
    a. Oxygen
    b. Fuel
    c. Hydraulic
    d. Electrical conduit

12. Which of these should not be used in a high-pressure system?
    a. Beaded fittings
    b. Flared fittings
    c. Flareless fittings
    d. Permanent fittings

Chapter 9
Fluid Lines and Fittings

MULTIPLE CHOICE
QUESTIONS

name:

date:

13. A fluid line with a label with four-pointed stars on it holds:
    a. Fuel
    b. Electricity
    c. Lubricant
    d. Hydraulic fluid

14. A fluid line with a label with circles on it holds:
    a. Fuel
    b. Electricity
    c. Lubricant
    d. Hydraulic fluid

15. Standard AN fittings made of aluminum are colored:
    a. Black
    b. Blue
    c. Natural
    d. Gray

16. What type of material is a fitting marked MS21911-6-D made of?
    a. Aluminum alloy
    b. Steel
    c. Brass
    d. Bronze

17. When replacing rigid tubing, why should you never select a path for the tubing that does not require bends in the tubing?
    a. A tube cannot be cut or flared accurately enough to be installed without bending and be free of mechanical strain.
    b. Bends permit the tube to expand and contract when the temperature changes.
    c. Bends absorb vibration.
    d. All the above

18. Which of these flexible tube materials has the best resistance to petroleum products?
    a. Buna-N
    b. Pure rubber
    c. Butyl
    d. Neoprene

19. Which of these types of flexible tube materials can be used for Skydrol?
    a. Butyl
    b. Teflon
    c. Buna-N
    d. Neoprene

20. When a flexible hose is repaired using existing hardware and new hose material, it should be tested before it is reinstalled. At what pressure should the hose be tested?
    a. At system pressure
    b. At three times system pressure
    c. At 1.5 times system pressure
    d. At two times system pressure

1. Describe how to cut a metal tube using a tube cutter.

ANALYSIS
QUESTIONS

name:

2. Some tube fittings have pipe threads and some have machine threads. What is the difference? What can each type be used for?

date:

3. Describe how swaged fittings work and where they are used.

4. What are some problems frequently found during rigid tube inspection, and how are they repaired?

ANALYSIS
QUESTIONS

name:

date:

5. What are some factors to consider when installing flexible hose assemblies?

1. The ________________________ is a record in which all data concerning an aircraft is recorded.

2. High-quality logbooks can mean a higher ________________________ for the aircraft.

3. An aircraft inspection checklist should include checking the batteries for proper installation and ________________________.

4. An aircraft inspection checklist should include checking the studs and nuts on the engine and nacelles for proper ________________________ and obvious defects.

5. The manufacturer's ________________________ contains complete instructions for maintaining all systems and components installed on the aircraft.

6. All work done on aircraft must comply with the ________________________, established by law to provide for the safe and orderly conduct of flight operations.

7. The FAA publishes ________________________ that make aircraft owners, operators, and technicians aware of potentially unsafe conditions or aircraft defects and how to correct them.

8. A/An ________________________ includes information on an aircraft's engine ratings, airspeed limits, center of gravity ranges, maximum weight, and other data.

9. The checklist for a preflight inspection can be found in the aircraft's ________________________.

10. According to Title 14 of the CFR, aircraft used for commercial purposes must have a complete inspection after every ________________________ hours of flight.

11. An annual inspection must be conducted by a certified airframe and powerplant maintenance technician with ________________________.

12. A/An ________________________ inspection program includes regular checks of routine items and inspections of detailed items and specific areas at times spread over a 12-month cycle.

13. The ________________________ standardized the format for presenting maintenance information in aircraft maintenance manuals, meaning a maintenance technician can always find information on a system in the same section of an aircraft maintenance manual, regardless of manufacturer.

14. In a special inspection after a heavy or rough landing, ________________________ is the most easily detected sign that excessive load was imposed during the landing.

FILL IN THE BLANK QUESTIONS

name:

date:

FILL IN THE BLANK
QUESTIONS

name:

date:

15. Damage from a/an _________________________ is more likely to occur in nonmetallic structures than in good electrical conductors such as aluminum or steel.

16. A/An _________________________ may be issued to allow a damaged or overdue-for-inspection aircraft to be flown to a base where repairs, alterations, or maintenance are to be performed.

17. _________________________ inspection or testing is used to determine the airworthiness of a component or part without damaging it.

18. A/An _________________________ is used to examine the inside of a reciprocating engine cylinder without disassembling the whole engine.

19. Nonporous materials can be checked for defects open to the surface through _________________________ inspection.

20. _________________________ inspection is an NDI technique that uses sound energy moving through the test specimen to detect flaws.

21. An ultrasonic test instrument requires access to (how many) _________________________ surface(s) of the material to be inspected.

22. _________________________ inspection is a method of detecting invisible cracks and other defects in ferromagnetic materials.

23. To locate a defect in a part, it is essential that the magnetic lines of force pass approximately _________________________ to the defect.

24. _________________________ inspection techniques are used to locate defects or flaws in airframe structures or engines with little or no disassembly.

25. A quick evaluation of any accessible surface to detect the presence of delamination or debonding in composite structures can be accomplished by _________________________.

26. In a butt weld, the penetration should be _________________________ percent of the thickness of the base metal.

1. Aircraft may be inspected using a calendar inspection system or according to:
   a. Flight hours
   b. Fuel usage
   c. The occurrence of events likely to damage the aircraft
   d. Random variation

2. Before starting an aircraft inspection:
   a. Open or remove all plates, access doors, fairings, and cowlings
   b. Review reference information on the aircraft being inspected
   c. Clean the aircraft structure
   d. All the above

3. Which of these items would not usually be part of an inspection checklist for the fuselage and hull?
   a. Fabric and skin
   b. Engine mount
   c. Envelope gas bags, ballast tanks, and related parts
   d. Systems and components

4. Which of these publications is likely to include new instructions on modifying, inspecting, or servicing a specific part of a specific type of aircraft?
   a. Maintenance Manual
   b. Code of Federal Regulations
   c. Manufacturers' Service Bulletin
   d. Airworthiness Directive

5. Which of these contains instructions for maintaining all the systems and components installed on an aircraft?
   a. Maintenance Manual
   b. Code of Federal Regulations
   c. Manufacturers' Service Bulletin
   d. Airworthiness Directive

6. Which of these provides instructions for repairing an airframe?
   a. Code of Federal Regulations
   b. Type Certificate Data Sheet
   c. Structural Repair Manual
   d. Illustrated Parts Catalogue

7. Which of these presents component breakdowns of structure and equipment in disassembly sequence?
   a. Code of Federal Regulations
   b. Type Certificate Data Sheet
   c. Structural Repair Manual
   d. Illustrated Parts Catalogue

8. Which of these does the FAA publish to notify aircraft owners and others of unsafe conditions and to prescribe the conditions under which the aircraft may continue to operate?
   a. Maintenance Manual
   b. Code of Federal Regulations
   c. Manufacturers' Service Bulletin
   d. Airworthiness Directive

9. Which of these publications shows the location of an aircraft's datum?
   a. Code of Federal Regulations
   b. Type Certificate Data Sheet
   c. Structural Repair Manual
   d. Illustrated Parts Catalogue

10. What type of inspection involves a walk-around to check the general condition of an aircraft as well as verification of fuel and oil levels as detailed in the pilot's operating handbook?
    a. Preflight Inspection
    b. 100-Hour Inspection
    c. Annual Inspection
    d. Progressive Inspection

11. Which of these divides inspection requirements into phases so as to avoid taking the aircraft out of service for an extended period?
    a. Preflight Inspection
    b. 100-Hour Inspection
    c. Annual Inspection
    d. Progressive Inspection

Chapter 10

Inspection Concepts and Techniques

MULTIPLE CHOICE
QUESTIONS

name:

date:

12. Aircraft with an air traffic control transponder must have the transponder inspected every:
    a. 12 months
    b. 24 months
    c. 6 months
    d. 100 flight hours

13. The emphasis of an inspection following a flight through severe turbulence should be on:
    a. Landing gear
    b. Fuel leakage along riveted seams
    c. Upper and lower wing surfaces, to check for excessive buckles or permanent wrinkles
    d. Static discharge wicks

14. Inspection of aerial application aircraft, like crop dusters, should take into account:
    a. The corrosive nature of the chemicals involved in the aircraft's tasks
    b. The typical flight profile of these aircraft
    c. High shear loading on skin rivets
    d. Both A and B

15. Which of these inspection methods requires applying a developer?
    a. Magnetic particle inspection
    b. Eddy current inspection
    c. Liquid penetrant inspection
    d. Ultrasonic inspection

16. Which inspection method uses an electromagnetic field to measure a difference in hardness rates within a metal part?
    a. Borescope inspection
    b. Eddy current inspection
    c. Liquid penetrant inspection
    d. Ultrasonic inspection

17. Which of these inspection methods detects flaws by measuring the amplitude of signals and the time required for signals to travel between the surface and the flaw?
    a. Magnetic particle inspection
    b. Eddy current inspection
    c. Liquid penetrant inspection
    d. Ultrasonic inspection

18. This inspection method involves placing sensors at various locations on an aircraft structure, applying a load or stress, and measuring the sound waves that are emitted by cracks or areas of corrosion.
    a. Acoustic emission testing
    b. Pulse echo testing
    c. Resonance testing
    d. Through transmission testing

19. This inspection method can detect cracks, laps, seams, cold shuts, inclusions, splits, tears, pipes, and voids inside or on the surface of metal aircraft parts.
    a. Magnetic particle inspection
    b. Eddy current inspection
    c. Acoustic emission testing
    d. Ultrasonic inspection

20. The induction of a magnetic field consisting of concentric circles of force about and within a metal part by passing electric current through the part is called:
    a. Longitudinal magnetization
    b. Solenoids
    c. Circular magnetization
    d. Flux direction

21. Magnetic particle inspection using a fluorescent solution and a black light is called:
    a. Demagnetization
    b. Continuous inspection method
    c. Residual inspection method
    d. Magnaglo inspection

22. Demagnetizing current should not be cut off until:
    a. The magnetic particles drop off the part
    b. The part is 1 to 2 feet from the solenoid coil
    c. The magnetometer reads zero or less
    d. A borescope reveals no residual magnetism

23. Which of these is not a factor in preparing for a radiographic exposure?
    a. Material thickness and density
    b. The exposure distance
    c. Temperature
    d. All the above factors must be considered

24. A gas cavity, as seen in a radiograph, looks like:
    a. A sphere
    b. A two-dimensional plane
    c. A line
    d. A white area

25. Electrical conductivity in a composite structure with embedded aluminum can be checked with:
    a. An ohmmeter
    b. A borescope
    c. A solenoid
    d. Fixed (nonportable) magnetizing apparatus

<u>Chapter 10</u>

Inspection Concepts and Techniques

MULTIPLE CHOICE QUESTIONS

name:

date:

1. When preparing for an inspection, what information would you look for in the aircraft's logbook? At the conclusion of an inspection, what information would you add to the aircraft's logbook?

Chapter 10

Inspection
Concepts and
Techniques

ANALYSIS
QUESTIONS

name:

date:

2. Describe the publications that provide information for aviation mechanics on operating and maintaining aircraft and related equipment.

ANALYSIS
QUESTIONS

name:

date:

3. Some inspections are done regularly according to the calendar or flight time systems. Others are recommended following certain events or operating conditions. What events or conditions indicate that a special inspection may be warranted?

4. Describe the process for performing a liquid penetrant inspection.

5. How do you prepare a part for magnetic particle inspection? What types of metals can interfere with magnetic particle testing?

1. _______________________ hammers should not be used for striking punch bolts, bolts, or nails.

2. A common screwdriver head should fill at least _______________________ of the screw slot.

3. A screw with a perfect cross on its recessed head should be tightened and loosened with a _______________________ screwdriver.

FILL IN THE BLANK QUESTIONS

name:

4. _______________________ pliers are used exclusively for twisting safety wiring.

5. _______________________ are used to locate centers for drawing circles, to start holes for drilling, and transfer the location of holes in patterns, among other uses.

date:

6. A/An _______________________ wrench is useful in close quarters because its head has 12 points and it can be used in places with as little as 15 degrees of swing.

7. A wrench with a detachable handle that fits differently sized heads is known as a _______________________ wrench.

8. A/An _______________________ wrench is a precision tool that indicates the amount of turning or twisting force being applied to a nut or bolt.

9. Cuts made with hand snips should be made _______________________ from the layout line and finished with hand filing because the snips create minute fractures along the cut.

10. _______________________ are used to square ends, round corners, remove burrs and slivers from metal, straighten uneven edges, and smooth rough edges.

11. The _______________________ of a twist drill bit fits into the chuck of a hand or power drill.

12. A/An _______________________ is used to smooth and enlarge holes to exact size.

13. To cut a cone-shaped depression around a hole to allow a rivet head or screw head to set flush with the surface of the material, use a/an _______________________.

14. If you need to cut threads on the inside of a hole, you could use a/an _______________________.

15. If you need to cut external threads on round stock, you could use a/an _______________________.

16. A/An _______________________ works like an ordinary tri-square, but its head slides along the blade and it includes a spirit level and scriber.

17. According to Figure 11-30, drill speeds are _______________________ when drilling soft metals than when drilling harder metals.

FILL IN THE BLANK
QUESTIONS

name:

date:

18. Outside ___________________ are used for measuring, for example, the diameter of a piece of round stock.

19. Some ___________________ display measurements on a digital liquid crystal display (LCD). They can measure to the thousandth or ten-thousandth of an inch.

20. On a micrometer equipped with a Vernier scale, the barrel scale reads 0.215 inches and the thimble scale reads 0.013 inches. If the Vernier scale's 4 is aligned with one of the marks on the thimble scale. The measurement is ___________________ inches.

1. This type of hammer should always be used when pounding a wood chisel or gouge.
   a. Wooden mallet
   b. Ball peen hammer
   c. Riveting hammer
   d. Cross peen hammer

2. Both ends of this type of screwdriver are bent 90 degrees to the shank handle.
   a. Phillips
   b. Reed & Prince
   c. Replaceable tip
   d. Offset

3. This type of screw has a cross with an enlarged center.
   a. Phillips
   b. Reed & Prince
   c. Replaceable tip
   d. Offset

4. This type of pliers can be used for cutting wire, rivets, and small screws.
   a. Roundnose
   b. Needlenose
   c. Diagonal
   d. Duckbill

5. Which of these is not a recommended use for a punch?
   a. Removing damaged rivets
   b. Cutting and chipping metal
   c. Punching holes in sheet metal
   d. Placing reference marks on metal

6. Which type of punch is used to knock out damaged rivets, pins, and bolts?
   a. Prick punch
   b. Center punch
   c. Drive punch
   d. Transfer punch

7. This type of box-end wrench can be swung back and forth, with force being exerted only during the swing in one direction.
   a. Ratcheting
   b. Combination
   c. Adjustable
   d. Allen

8. Use this type of wrench on a round nut with notches cut in the outer edge.
   a. Allen
   b. Hook spanner
   c. Flare nut
   d. Strap

9. Use this type of wrench to grip or rotate a round or irregularly shaped component such as a pipe or tube.
   a. Allen
   b. Hook spanner
   c. Flare nut
   d. Strap

10. Headless setscrews can be installed and removed with this type of wrench.
    a. Allen
    b. Hook spanner
    c. Flare nut
    d. Strap

11. The preferred hacksaw blade for cutting solid-stock aluminum has how many teeth per inch?
    a. 14
    b. 18
    c. 24
    d. 32

12. A chisel is made of hard steel and can be used to cut and chip:
    a. Aluminum or tin
    b. Tungsten
    c. Any metal softer than the chisel itself
    d. Plastic or hard rubber

<u>Chapter 11</u>

Hand Tools and Measuring Devices

MULTIPLE CHOICE QUESTIONS

name:

date:

MULTIPLE CHOICE
QUESTIONS

name:

date:

13. This kind of file is usually single cut, rectangular, used for drawfiling, and tapered slightly in thickness and width for about one-third of its length.
   a. Flat file
   b. Rattail file
   c. Warding file
   d. Mill file

14. What type of drill should you use around flammable materials?
   a. Electric drill
   b. Pneumatic drill
   c. Twist drill
   d. Reamer

15. The drill bits for a machine shop drill press usually have what kind of shank?
   a. Straight
   b. Square
   c. Tapered
   d. Left

16. If you plan to ream a hole to exact size, it should be drilled undersize by how much?
   a. 3 to 7 thousandths of an inch
   b. 3 to 7 hundredths of an inch
   c. 3 to 7 tenths of an inch
   d. 0.0003 to 0.0007 inch

17. A No. 35 twist drill has a diameter of:
   a. 0.0960 inch
   b. 0.1360 inch
   c. 0.1100 inch
   d. 0.5100 inch

18. What kind of tap is used first?
   a. Plug
   b. Bottoming
   c. Taper
   d. National Fine

19. This tool is used to scribe circles and arcs and to transfer measurements from a rule to the work.
   a. Scriber
   b. Divider or pencil compass
   c. Caliper
   d. Micrometer

20. What type of calipers would you use to measure the distance between two surfaces, the width of a slot, or the diameter of the interior of a pipe?
   a. Outside
   b. Inside
   c. Hermaphrodite
   d. Slide

1. What are some ways you can avoid damaging a screw head when installing or removing the screw?

2. Describe how to set up and use a hacksaw to cut metal.

3. What is the difference between crossfiling and drawfiling?

Chapter 11

Hand Tools and Measuring Devices

ANALYSIS
QUESTIONS

name:

date:

ANALYSIS
QUESTIONS

name:

date:

4. Explain the systems for indicating the diameter of a drill bit. There are three.

5. Describe how to cut threads on the inside of a hole.

Fundamentals of Electricity and Electronics

FILL IN THE BLANK QUESTIONS

name:

date:

1. A/An _________________ is a chemical combination of two or more elements.

2. At the center of an atom is the nucleus, which contains positively charged _________________ and neutrally charged neutrons.

3. A/An _________________ undergoes the change during chemical reactions because of its position at the distant periphery of the atom relative to the nucleus.

4. The maximum number of electrons that can be contained in the third energy level or shell is _________________.

5. An atom that has gained one or more extra electrons is called a/an _________________.

6. Elements such as gold, copper, and silver possess many free electrons and thus make good _________________.

7. _________________ charges repel each other.

8. The field of force that exists around a charged body is called a/an _________________ field.

9. In diagrams, the direction of the field around a positive charge is always _________________ from the charge.

10. One of the most frequent causes of damage to a solid-state component or integrated circuits is the _________________ from the human body when one of these devices is handled.

11. Three _________________ materials—nickel, cobalt, and gadolinium—are magnetic to a certain degree.

12. Materials such as soft iron and other ferrous metals are said to have _________________, the measure of ease with which magnetic flux can penetrate a material.

13. If a conductor wire is grasped in the left hand with the thumb pointing in the direction of the current flow, the fingers will be wrapped around the conductor in the same direction as the lines of the current-induced _________________.

14. The combination of an iron core in a coil of wire loops is called a/an _________________, since the ends of the coil possess the characteristics of a bar magnet.

15. A/An _________________ operates on the principle that an iron core, spring loaded off center in a coil, will be rapidly pulled into the center position when the coil is energized.

FILL IN THE BLANK
QUESTIONS

name:

date:

16. Electrons move, when a path is available, from a point of excess electrons to a point deficient in electrons, and the force that causes this movement is the ___________________: that is, the potential difference in electrical energy between the two points.

17. One _______________ of current is equivalent to one coulomb of charge passing through a conductor in one second.

18. If you double the resistance of a conductor, the current is _______________.

19. The resistance of a metal conductor is directly proportional to its _______________.

20. Electrical power is measured in _______________.

21. When current flows through a resistive circuit, energy is dissipated in the form of _______________.

22. A rheostat is a type of _______________ resistor.

23. A/An _______________ occurs when some point in a circuit, where full system voltage is present, comes in direct contact with the ground or return side of the circuit.

24. Magnetic and thermal overload are two types of _______________ used in aircraft systems.

25. The direct current through a/an _______________ will always be the same through every element and at any point.

26. The sum of all voltages around a closed direct current path or loop is _______________.

27. Voltage _______________ make it possible to obtain more than one voltage from a single power source.

28. The primary difference between a series circuit and a/an _______________ circuit is that more than one path is provided for the current in the latter.

29. The sum of the currents into a junction (a point in the circuit where two or more circuit paths come together) _______________ the sum of the currents flowing out of that same junction.

30. _______________changes direction at regular intervals: it increases in value at a definite rate from zero to a maximum positive strength, then decreases back to zero, then reverses direction, similarly increasing from zero to maximum positive strength and decreasing to zero.

31. Moving a/an _________________________ through a conductor induces an electromagnetic force in the conductor.

32. The frequency is the number of cycles of alternating current per second, and the standard unit of frequency measure is the _________________________.

33. The basic unit of capacitance is the _________________________.

34. The number of turns in the winding and the core material determine the capacity of a/an _________________________.

35. _________________________ is the combined effects of resistance, inductive reactance, and capacitive reactance to oppose the current flow in an AC circuit.

36. A/An _________________________ changes electrical energy of a given voltage into electrical energy at a different voltage.

37. A multirange ammeter is usable over a wide range of voltages because each range uses a different _________________________.

38. The _________________________ is a high-range ohmmeter containing a hand-operated generator.

39. A DC meter, such as an ammeter, connected in an AC circuit will indicate _________________________.

40. A/An _________________________ circuit is a circuit that is not a complete or continuous path; it represents an infinitely large resistance.

41. When an ohmmeter is properly connected across a circuit component and a resistance reading is obtained, the component _________________________.

42. The _________________________, which has characteristics similar to an electrolytic cell, is the most common type of primary-cell battery.

43. A/An _________________________ is any kind of electrolytic cell in which the electrochemical reaction that releases energy is reversible.

44. Batteries are charged by either the constant current or the constant voltage method. A battery installed in an aircraft is charged using direct current from the aircraft generator system using the _________________________ method.

45. A/An _________________________ is used in some aircraft systems to convert a portion of the aircraft's DC power to AC power.

46. The process of adding small amounts of impurities to a semiconductor material to increase current flow is called _________________________.

FILL IN THE BLANK QUESTIONS

name:

date:

FILL IN THE BLANK
QUESTIONS

name:

date:

47. PN junction diodes will offer very little resistance to current in a/an ___________________________ diode.

48. A/An ___________________ is a device that transforms alternating current into direct current by limiting or regulating the direction of current flow.

49. A/An ___________________ is a three-terminal device primarily used to amplify signals and control current within a circuit.

50. The three basic configurations of a transistor are common-emitter, common-base, and common-___________________. The term "common" is used to indicate which element of the transistor is common to both the input and output.

51. The use of vacuum tubes in aircraft has declined lately because of the many advantages of ___________________.

52. Both inductors and capacitors can be used as ___________________, with the inductors offering high impedance to the ripple frequency and the capacitor offering very low impedance.

53. A/An ___________________ is a device that enables an input signal to control an output signal, with the output signal generally being of greater magnitude than the input signal.

54. ___________________ is measured by dividing the output signal by the input signal.

55. Autopilot amplifiers take the ___________________ from the flight guidance system and amplify the signals to a level usable for driving the servo motors.

56. ___________________ occurs when a small portion of the output signal is sent back to the input signal to the amplifier and is out of phase with the input signal, degenerating the input signal.

57. In a logic circuit, when a signal that activates a circuit to 1 has an electrical level that is positive compared to the 0 condition, the ___________________ is said to be positive.

58. ___________________, a symbolic system used in representing the truth values of statements, is used in the binary system in digital computers mainly because the only truth values (true and false) can be represented by the binary digits (1 and 0).

59. The operation of a/an ___________________ is such that the output is high only when all of the inputs are high, and low whenever one or more inputs are low.

60. If current is collected from a generator using a commutator, it is ___________________ current.

61. The major parts of a DC generator are the field frame (or yoke), a rotating _______________________, and a brush assembly.

62. The speed—usually about 1,500 rpm—at which aircraft generators begin to produce their normal voltage is called the _______________________ speed.

63. Conductors carrying current in the same direction tend to be _______________________.

64. The amount of _______________________ developed in a coil varies by the strength of the magnetic field, the number of turns in the coil, and the position of the coil in the field.

65. In a/an _______________________ DC motor, the same current flowing through the field winding also flows through the armature winding.

66. In a/an _______________________ motor, the direction of rotation of the armature can be reversed by a single pole, double throw switch that directs the current through one of the two windings on the same pole.

67. Two types of AC motors are used in aircraft systems: _______________________ and synchronous motors.

68. The stationary portion of an AC motor is called a/an _______________________.

69. In a synchronous motor, alternating current is applied to the stator windings, producing a rotating magnetic field, and _______________________ is applied to rotor windings, creating another magnetic field. The two fields react to each other in such a way that the rotor is dragged along and rotates at the same speed as the rotating magnetic field produced by the stator windings.

70. A/An _______________________ motor is not self-starting, and all such motors require some sort of starting device—another motor or a second squirrel cage–type winding on the rotor, for example.

71. A/An _______________________ is a generator that produces alternating current.

72. The _______________________ type of alternator is used almost universally in aircraft systems, and the revolving armature type is generally not used.

73. A/An _______________________ is more commonly found on turbine powered aircraft. It regulates and protects the DC generation system.

<u>Chapter 12</u>

Fundamentals of Electricity and Electronics

FILL IN THE BLANK QUESTIONS

name:

date:

FILL IN THE BLANK
QUESTIONS

name:

date:

74. The speed of alternators must be constant, but the speed of an airplane engine varies. A hydraulic _________________________ drive is used on large multi-engine aircraft to deliver a constant output to an alternator.

75. In a hydraulic transmission connecting the aircraft engine and the generator, pistons in the cylinder assembly can be forced outward against the pushrod, which is pushed against the pump _________________________.

MULTIPLE CHOICE
QUESTIONS

name:

date:

1. The neutron has approximately the same mass as the:
    a. Proton
    b. Electron
    c. Nucleus
    d. An oxygen atom

2. Electrons that can participate in chemical bonds with other atoms are called:
    a. Ions
    b. Free electrons
    c. Valence electrons
    d. Shell electrons

3. Materials such as glass and ceramic that conduct electrical current poorly are called:
    a. Conductors
    b. Insulators
    c. Ions
    d. Semiconductors

4. The imaginary lines drawn to illustrate the field around a charged body:
    a. Are always drawn pointing away from a positive charge
    b. Are always drawn pointing toward the positive charge
    c. Can be drawn in any direction, since they're imaginary
    d. Are always drawn using dotted lines

5. Which of these statements about magnetism is not true?
    a. Magnetism is an invisible force.
    b. The nature of magnetism is completely understood by scientists.
    c. Each molecule that makes up a magnetic iron bar is itself a tiny magnet with both north and south poles.
    d. The earth is a giant magnet.

6. Soft iron can be used to shield an instrument from a magnetic field because the force prefers the metal's low level of opposition as opposed to air, a quality known as:
    a. Insularity
    b. Polarity
    c. Reluctance
    d. Retentivity

7. The strength of an electromagnet's magnetic field can be increased by:
    a. Increasing the flow of current
    b. Increasing the number of loops in the wire
    c. Decreasing the number of loops in the wire
    d. Both A and B

8. Electromotive force is better known as:
    a. Current
    b. Voltage
    c. Resistance
    d. Charge

9. A measurement of the rate at which a charge (i.e., free electrons) flows through a conductor is:
    a. Current
    b. Voltage
    c. Resistance
    d. Charge

10. If the resistance in a conductor is doubled, the current will be:
    a. One-quarter of its original value
    b. Also doubled
    c. Cut in half
    d. Quadrupled

11. If the cross-sectional area of a conductor is doubled, resistance to current flow will be:
    a. One-quarter of its original value
    b. Also doubled
    c. Cut in half
    d. Quadrupled

12. If 400 J of energy is consumed in 5 seconds, the power is:
    a. 80 watts
    b. 80 joules
    c. 2,000 watts
    d. 1 horsepower

MULTIPLE CHOICE
QUESTIONS

name:

date:

13. If a circuit has a known voltage of 12 volts and a resistance of 8 ohms, the power in the circuit is:
    a. 1.5 watts
    b. 12 watts
    c. 18 watts
    d. 96 watts

14. Batteries are the most common example of this source of electricity:
    a. Pressure source
    b. Chemical source
    c. Thermal source
    d. Light source

15. A resistor with a brown band, a black band, a red band, and a gold band:
    a. Has a resistance value of 10 ohms and a tolerance of 20 percent
    b. Has a resistance value of 10 ohms and a tolerance of 5 percent
    c. Has a resistance value of 100 ohms and a tolerance of 9 percent
    d. Has a resistance value of 1,000 ohms and a tolerance of 5 percent

16. A variable resistor whose resistance decreases as the sensed temperature increases is called a/an:
    a. Linear potentiometer
    b. Rheostat
    c. Thermistor
    d. Photoconductive cell

17. A circuit protection device that can be reset rather than replaced after it opens a circuit in over-current conditions is:
    a. Circuit breaker
    b. Fuse
    c. Current limiter
    d. Direct short

18. Ignition switches and voltmeter switches are typically this kind of switch:
    a. Double-pole, single-throw
    b. Microswitch
    c. Lighted pushbutton switch
    d. Rotary selector switch

19. A series DC circuit with a current of 0.2 A includes three resistors: 500 ohm, 200 ohm, and 300 ohm. What is the source voltage?
    a. 100 V
    b. 200 V
    c. 500 V
    d. 1,000 V

20. A series DC circuit has a current of 250 mA. The source voltage is 70. There are three resistors of known value—20 ohm, 50 ohm, and 80 ohm—and one resistor whose value is unknown. What is the voltage drop across the fourth resistor?
    a. 100 ohms
    b. 200 ohms
    c. 500 ohms
    d. 1,000 ohms

21. What is the total resistance in a parallel DC circuit when there are two resistors (300 ohm and 500 ohm), with one resistor on each branch of the circuit?
    a. 100 ohms
    b. 0.005 ohm
    c. 187.5 ohms
    d. 400 ohms

22. Which of these statements comparing AC and DC is not true?
    a. DC flows constantly in one direction, while AC changes direction at regular intervals.
    b. AC motors are generally smaller and simpler than DC motors.
    c. The waveforms of AC and DC are identical.
    d. All three statements are true.

23. Which of these is not a factor in the value of the electromotive force induced by a loop conductor rotating in a magnetic field?
    a. The number of wires moving through the magnetic field
    b. The strength of the magnetic field
    c. The speed of rotation
    d. The direction of rotation

24. The time required for a sine wave to complete one full cycle is called a/an:
    a. Period
    b. Cycle
    c. Wave
    d. Frequency

25. To be in phase, two waveforms must:
    a. Follow the same pattern
    b. Be designated as either "leading" or "lagging"
    c. Reach their minimum and maximum points at the same time
    d. Reach their minimum and maximum points at the same time and in the same direction

26. Most AC voltmeters display the root mean square of the maximum current, or:
    a. The instantaneous value
    b. The peak value
    c. The effective value
    d. Capacitance

27. A component constructed of two parallel plates separated by a nonconducting dielectric that serves as a reservoir for electricity is called a:
    a. Capacitor
    b. Resistor
    c. Transistor
    d. Semiconductor

28. What is the total capacitance in a simple series circuit that contains these capacitors: 8 µF, 6 µF, and 4 µF?
    a. 18 µF
    b. 1.85 µF
    c. 0.542 µF
    d. 0.055 µF

29. Inductance is measured in:
    a. Henries
    b. Betsies
    c. Farads
    d. Amperes

30. What is the inductive reactance in an AC series circuit where the inductance is 0.165 henry and the voltage is 110 volts at a frequency of 75 cycles per second?
    a. 1,237.50 ohms
    b. 77.72 ohms
    c. 1,361.25 ohms
    d. 0.24 ohm

31. What is the total impedance in an AC series circuit where the voltage is 110 volts at 60 cycles per second, there is a coil with an inductance of 0.25 henry, and there is a lamp with 10 ohms resistance?
    a. 13.74 ohms
    b. 15.23 ohms
    c. 188.74 ohms
    d. 4.41 ohms

32. In an AC circuit, the product of the volts and amperes is the:
    a. Apparent power
    b. Actual power
    c. True power
    d. Transformative power

33. Which of these is not one of the basic parts of a transformer?
    a. An iron core
    b. A dielectric
    c. A primary winding
    d. A secondary winding

34. If 24 volts are applied to a transformer where the primary winding has 15 turns and the secondary winding has 5 turns, and the transformer is 100 percent efficient, what is the output voltage?
    a. 4 volts
    b. 6 volts
    c. 72 volts
    d. 8 volts

35. Which of these cannot be used to measure both AC and DC current?
    a. Electrodynamometer
    b. D'Arsonval meter
    c. Moving iron vane meter
    d. All three of these can measure both AC and DC current.

Chapter 12

Fundamentals of Electricity and Electronics

MULTIPLE CHOICE
QUESTIONS

name:

date:

36. A device that uses a CRT to display and quantify various waveform characteristics such as phase relationships, amplitudes, and durations is:
    a. Oscilloscope
    b. Wattmeter
    c. Varmeter
    d. Methoscope

37. A lead-acid car battery is what type of battery?
    a. Primary cell
    b. Single cell
    c. Latent cell
    d. Secondary cell

38. Comparing the two main types of inverters, which of these is true?
    a. Static inverters are considerably smaller, more compact, and lighter than rotary inverters.
    b. Rotary inverters are considerably smaller, more compact, and lighter than inductor-type inverters.
    c. Static inverters use a permanent magnet, but a rotary inverter never does.
    d. Static inverters have a long warm-up period compared to the warm-up period for a rotary inverter.

39. The preferred material used in semiconductors is silicon. The reason for this is:
    a. Silicon atoms form ionic bonds that are difficult to break.
    b. Two silicon atoms each provide one electron to share with the other, creating a covalent bond that is stable and requires much energy to break.
    c. Because of the term "Silicon Valley."
    d. The outer shell of the atom contains spaces to receive electrons driven by a current.

40. A diode that will break down when the circuit potential is equal to or in excess of the desired reverse bias voltage is:
    a. A photodiode
    b. A Schottky diode
    c. A power rectifier diode
    d. A Zener diode

41. A transistor where the input signal is applied to the base and the output signal is taken from the emitter has a/an:
    a. Common-collector configuration
    b. Common-base configuration
    c. Common-emitter configuration
    d. PNP configuration

42. Typically, after an AC signal has been rectified, the pulses of voltage are changed to a usable form of DC by means of:
    a. Attenuation
    b. Frequency response
    c. Filtering
    d. Inductance

43. The most efficient class of amplifier is:
    a. Class A
    b. Class AB
    c. Class B
    d. Class C

44. In a logic circuit, a two-input gate that has a low output only when both inputs are high is symbolized by:
    a. AND
    b. NAND
    c. OR
    d. NOR

45. The position where the brushes in a DC generator are placed to prevent a short or sparking is called the:
    a. Neural plane
    b. Position D
    c. Neutral plane
    d. Field frame

46. An inspection of a DC generator system should include which of the following checks:
    a. Security of generator mountings
    b. Voltage regulator operation
    c. Condition of generator brushes
    d. All the above

47. When the amount of current flowing through the field windings of a DC motor is increased:
    a. The motor slows down
    b. The motor speeds up
    c. The counter electromotive force decreases
    d. Resistance decreases

48. The most common type of alternator in the electrical systems of an aircraft is:
    a. Single phase
    b. Two phase
    c. Three phase
    d. Six phase

49. The frequency of a six-pole, 600-rpm alternator is:
    a. 30 cps
    b. 3,600 cps
    c. 120 cps
    d. 600 cps

50. Which of these is frequently used in aircraft alternator systems to control alternator output?
    a. Overspeed circuit
    b. Transistorized voltage regulator
    c. Frequency regulator
    d. Bridge circuit

Chapter 12

Fundamentals of Electricity and Electronics

MULTIPLE CHOICE QUESTIONS

name:

date:

Fundamentals of Electricity and Electronics

ANALYSIS
QUESTIONS

name:

date:

1. How do the number and arrangement of electrons in an atom of an element influence whether the element is a conductor, insulator, or semiconductor?

2. Describe the difference between voltage and current.

3. What are four factors that affect the resistance of a conductor? What is the relationship between resistance, voltage, and current?

Fundamentals of Electricity and Electronics

ANALYSIS
QUESTIONS

name:

date:

4. What are some devices that protect against direct shorts and how do they work?

5. In a DC series circuit, how can different voltages be obtained from a single power source?

6. What are the advantages of alternating current over direct current, especially in aircraft?

7. Explain inductive reactance and capacitive reactance in an AC circuit, and the effect each has on the phase relationship between voltage and current.

8. Explain how you would construct a step-down transformer to change an input of 1,000 V to an output of 200 V.

9. What instruments can you use to check voltage, current, and resistance in a circuit? How are these items connected to the circuit?

Chapter 12

Fundamentals of Electricity and Electronics

ANALYSIS
QUESTIONS

name:

date:

ANALYSIS
QUESTIONS

name:

date:

10. How does a lead-acid battery produce voltage?

11. Most semiconductors are made of silicon—but not entirely of silicon. What characteristics of silicon make it a good insulator and bad conductor, and what must be done to silicon to increase its conductivity and to create a usable semiconductor?

12. Describe a logic circuit where an indicator light would be lit when either the forward or aft cabin door is open and the braking system is engaged. (Obviously, this is not a realistic situation, but rather an example.) Include logic polarity and gates in your response.

13. Describe the basic parts of a simple DC generator and how it generates DC voltage.

<u>Chapter 12</u>

Fundamentals of Electricity and Electronics

ANALYSIS
QUESTIONS

name:

date:

14. What is the difference between a generator and a motor?

15. What are some tasks involved in alternator system maintenance?

Mechanic Privileges and Limitations

1. The federal regulation that governs the certification of airmen other than flight crew members is ________________________.

2. A fundamental difference between a mechanic certificate and a repairman certificate is that the mechanic certificate is ____________________, meaning its issue is not tied to the location and firm at which the certificated employee works.

3. FAA Form ________________ is used to apply for an airman certificate and/or rating.

FILL IN THE BLANK QUESTIONS

name:

4. A conviction on federal or state ____________________________ can lead to an airman certificate being denied or suspended.

5. The minimum score on the required airman knowledge tests is ____________________.

date:

6. Assuming that the mechanic has recent work experience, his or her mechanic certificate is effective until it is ________________________, suspended, or revoked.

7. The FAA recognizes two ratings on mechanic certificates: airframe and ________________________.

8. An applicant for a mechanic certificate must show that he or she has a minimum of ________________________ of practical experience related to the rating being sought, or 30 months of experience if applying for certification with both ratings.

9. A certificated mechanic is not permitted to perform major repair or major alteration to ________________________ nor perform any repair or alteration to instruments. This work is reserved for certificated repairmen at authorized repair stations.

10. A mechanic with an airframe rating may approve and return to service an airframe, appliance, or related part after he or she has performed, supervised, or inspected ________________________ repairs or alterations.

11. A mechanic with both ratings may apply for ____________________________ if he or she has held the certificate for at least three years and been active for the last two years.

12. ________________________ is the study of standards of conduct and moral judgment.

Chapter 13

Mechanic Privileges and Limitations

MULTIPLE CHOICE
QUESTIONS

name:

date:

1. The certification of maintenance technicians is regulated by which portion of 14 CFR 65?
   a. Subpart A
   b. Subpart B
   c. Subpart C
   d. Subpart D

2. The revocation of a mechanic certificate means that the person who held it cannot apply for another certificate within:
   a. 6 months
   b. 9 months
   c. 1 year
   d. 3 years

3. A temporary mechanic certificate may be issued when the applicant passes all required tests. The temporary certificate is valid for up to:
   a. 120 days
   b. 90 days
   c. 60 days
   d. 30 days

4. Which of these activities during mechanic certificate testing can lead to the guilty party's not being eligible for any certificate for the next year?
   a. Copying the test
   b. Giving help to someone else during the test taking period
   c. Receiving help from someone else during the test taking period
   d. Any of these

5. If you fail the mechanic certificate test, how long must you wait before you are eligible to try again?
   a. 1 week
   b. 30 days
   c. 6 months
   d. 1 year

6. Which of the following tests are maintenance technicians required to submit to, according to federal regulations?
   a. Urine test
   b. Breath test
   c. Both A and B
   d. None

7. Which of the following is not required to be eligible for a mechanic certificate?
   a. Be at least 21 years of age
   b. Be able to read, write, speak and understand English
   c. Passing all required tests within the preceding 24 months
   d. Demonstrate the appropriate knowledge and skills for the certificate rating being sought

8. A person who holds an A&P rating has passed the application and testing process for:
   a. Aircraft rating and propeller rating
   b. Airframe rating and powerplant rating
   c. Airframe rating, powerplant rating, and mechanic certificate
   d. Airframe rating, powerplant rating, and inspection authorization

9. Basic principles for installing and maintaining propellers are included in the testing for:
   a. Powerplant rating
   b. Airframe rating
   c. Mechanic certification
   d. Light sport rating

10. Which of these activities is a certificated mechanic authorized to perform?
    a. Major alterations to propellers
    b. Preventive maintenance
    c. Alteration to instruments
    d. Authorize an aircraft for return to service

11. To keep using an A&P certificate, the holder must have been actively working as a mechanic for at least:
    a. 6 of the preceding 24 months
    b. 12 of the preceding 24 months
    c. 3 of the preceding 12 months
    d. 6 of the preceding 12 months

Chapter 13
Mechanic Privileges and Limitations

MULTIPLE CHOICE
QUESTIONS

name:

date:

12. Which of these is not a requirement to apply for an inspection authorization?
    a. Holding an A&P certificate for at least three years, and working actively for the last two years
    b. Complete at least 12 hours of additional preparatory coursework
    c. Have a fixed base of operation
    d. Have access to equipment, facilities, and data necessary to perform inspections and approve items for return to service

13. An inspection authorization expires March 31 of each odd numbered year. It may be renewed in which of the following ways?
    a. Performance of at least one annual inspection for each 90 days the technician has held the inspection authorization
    b. Successful completion of at least 8 hours of refresher courses
    c. Perform or supervise at least one progressive inspection
    d. Any of these will suffice

14. Which of the following is true regarding ethical behavior in the workplace?
    a. Unethical behavior tends to benefit the company that supports it.
    b. Giving an estimate that you know to be false is OK, because otherwise it would mean a loss of business and possibly of your job.
    c. Ethical behavior is not about monetary gain.
    d. Shoddy workmanship is illegal, but not unethical.

15. If you go along with unethical activities because of pressure from your bosses or supervisors, you should assume:
    a. That no one will ever find out
    b. That there is no guarantee that the person who asked you to participate in the activity will back you up in an investigation or court proceeding
    c. That the boss wouldn't have asked you if he or she didn't think it was in the company's best interest
    d. That you are blameless because you were just following orders

1. When are you not eligible to apply for a mechanic certificate or rating?

2. What tasks are you allowed to perform as a certificated mechanic with an airframe rating? What are you not allowed to do?

3. How can you obtain an inspection authorization, and how can you keep it?

Chapter 13
Mechanic Privileges and Limitations

ANALYSIS
QUESTIONS

name:

date:

Chapter 13
Mechanic Privileges and Limitations

ANALYSIS
QUESTIONS

name:

date:

4. Describe a situation in which you were forced to choose between ethical and unethical behavior. (If you can't think of one, invent one.) What did you choose to do, and on what factors was your decision based? What would the consequences have been if you had made the other choice, and what if any were the consequences following the choice you did make?

1.   It is generally agreed that _______________ percent of maintenance errors involve human factors.

2.   Approximately _______________________ percent of all aviation accidents are the result of human error.

3.   An error of _____________________ involves performing a task incorrectly.

4.   Complacency, distraction, fatigue, and pressure are some of the human factors that directly _______________________ many aviation accidents.

5.   The study and application of human factors is complex because there is not just _________________________________ to change how people are affected by certain conditions.

6.   _______________________ focuses on the mental well-being of the individual.

7.   Anthropometry is the study of the dimensions and abilities of the _______________________.

8.   The relations between people and work are the subject of a field of study called _______________________.

9.   The _______________________ system, developed in the early 1900s to reduce errors during medical procedures, is used in aviation today; for example, pilots are required to read back instructions or clearances given by air traffic control.

10. Human factors awareness in aviation maintenance, starting in the 1990s, stressed communication and _______________________.

11. The acronym _______________________ can help you remember the things we should be concerned about when considering aviation maintenance human factors.

12. Since physical and mental fatigue can increase errors, it is important to plan _______________________ when designing a job.

13. Human factors programs must be concerned with two types of environments: the _______________________ workplace in the hangar or in the shop, and the _______________________ environment that exists in the company.

14. _______________________ is the standerd human factors approach to identify the knowledge, skills, and attitudes necessary to perform each task in a given job.

15. The _________________________________ system, developed by Boeing, is used to investigate accidents and understand their root causes and contributing factors rather than to assign blame to maintenance personnel.

FILL IN THE BLANK QUESTIONS

name:

date:

16. The _________________________ model, developed by a consultant to KLM, considers the effect of procedures, machines, environment, and other personnel on the maintenance worker in order to determine the cause or causes of problems.

17. The _________________________ was introduced in 1990 and attempts to show how various holes in different systems must be aligned for an error to occur.

18. Human error is not avoidable, but it is _________________________.

19. A/An _________________________ is the specific individual activity that is an obvious event.

20. Twelve human factors essential to aircraft maintenance proficiency were compiled by Transport Canada in the early 1990s in a list known throughout the industry as "_________________________."

21. One way to prevent _________________________ in your job is to always expect to find something wrong.

22. It is estimated that _________________________ percent of maintenance-related errors are caused by distractions.

23. Since many maintenance tasks involve multiple technicians working together, a lack of _________________________ can lead to substandard outcomes.

24. Never replace a part with one that is not _________________________ for the sake of getting the job done.

25. _________________________ is the ability to express your feelings, opinions, beliefs, and needs in a positive, productive manner and should not be confused with being aggressive.

26. Temperature, noise, and poor lighting are _________________________ stressors that can lead to underperformance.

27. In a survey conducted by the United Kingdom Civil Aviation Authority, the most common aircraft maintenance error is the _________________________.

28. Historically, _________________________ percent of all accidents are caused by a machine failure, and _________________________ percent of all accidents are caused by human factors.

Chapter 14

Human
Factors

MULTIPLE CHOICE
QUESTIONS

name:

date:

1. Human factors applies to:
   a. Proper actions and improper actions
   b. Improper actions only
   c. Proper actions only
   d. Human error

2. The unintentional act of performing a task incorrectly that could degrade the system is called:
   a. Extraneous action
   b. Proper action
   c. Catastrophic error
   d. Human error

3. Laboratory studies that measure performance, productivity, or deficiencies come under a human factors discipline called:
   a. Clinical psychology
   b. Cognitive science
   c. Organizational psychology
   d. Experimental psychology

4. A human factors discipline that studies how our minds process information is:
   a. Computer science
   b. Cognitive science
   c. Organizational psychology
   d. Experimental psychology

5. A person who reviews an early design of a system, analyzes it for faults that can occur, and proposes changes to the design to promote a more healthy work environment is a:
   a. Safety engineer
   b. Anthropometrist
   c. Supervisor
   d. OSHA inspector

6. Someone who studies work, the reasonableness of work standards, and data on work performance might be a/an:
   a. Educational psychologist
   b. Industrial engineer
   c. AMT
   d. Physiologist

7. While other inventors focused on stable flight, Orrville and Wilbur Wright developed prototype flying machines that included:
   a. Practical interactive controls for pitch, roll, and yaw
   b. A seat belt
   c. An angle-of-attack sensor
   d. All of the above

8. The Hawthorne Effect suggests that:
   a. Certain individuals are suited only to certain aviation jobs.
   b. Machines are much more important than pilots.
   c. Motivational factors have a significant influence on human performance.
   d. Resources are necessary to complete a job.

9. Which of these items is not part of the acronym PEAR?
   a. People who do the job
   b. Environment in which they work
   c. Aviation parts and services
   d. Resources necessary to perform the job

10. Weather, workplace, personnel, pressures, and morale all fall under the PEAR heading of:
    a. People
    b. Environment
    c. Actions
    d. Resources

11. Anything a technician needs to get a job done—protective clothing, a tool, a fastener—is considered a/an:
    a. Human error
    b. Fixture
    c. Resource
    d. Skill

12. A technician misreads a work card and uses the wrong size rivet for a job. This is an example of what kind of error?
    a. Latent
    b. Active
    c. Intentional
    d. Unintentional

MULTIPLE CHOICE
QUESTIONS

name:

date:

13. A broken tool is put away without being fixed. A few weeks later, another technician attempts to use the tool and bruises his hand. Identify the latent error.
    a. Using a broken tool
    b. Bruising his hand
    c. The broken tool itself
    d. Failing to complete the job

14. According to the Model of Accident Causation, putting the wrong type of fuel in an aircraft would be:
    a. A latent failure
    b. An active failure
    c. A software failure
    d. An environmental failure

15. Which of the following does not belong in the "Dirty Dozen" list of factors negatively affecting human factors?
    a. Attention to safety
    b. Lack of resources
    c. Stress
    d. Lack of awareness

16. This "Dirty Dozen" human factor error is likely to occur across a shift change.
    a. Complacency
    b. Lack of awareness
    c. Lack of communication
    d. Lack of knowledge

17. When performing a routine task that one has done successfully many times before, one should guard against:
    a. Complacency
    b. Lack of awareness
    c. Lack of communication
    d. Pressure

18. This human factor consideration reduces cognitive ability, reaction time, coordination, and a person's ability to focus.
    a. Lack of communication
    b. Lack of resources
    c. Fatigue
    d. Lack of teamwork

19. Shift work can degrade performance because it requires technicians to work during low cycles in their natural:
    a. CFR
    b. Circadian rhythm
    c. Blood pressure
    d. Mood swings

20. Federal regulations require only this many hours of time off during a week of work.
    a. 40
    b. 80
    c. 24
    d. 42

21. The ability to positively and productively express your feelings, opinions, beliefs, and needs is called:
    a. Assertiveness
    b. Agressiveness
    c. Apologia
    d. Anthropometry

22. Lack of sleep, not eating properly, and poor physical condition are:
    a. Physical stressors
    b. Psychological stressors
    c. Physiological stressors
    d. Organizational stressors

23. When faced with a new or ambiguous situation at work, an individual's response is formed in large part by this frame of reference:
    a. Norms, or the way things are normally done
    b. Psychological stress
    c. Awareness
    d. Complacency

24. Which of these errors is not among the eight most common errors found in a study by the United Kingdom Civil Aviation Authority?
    a. Failure to secure access panels
    b. Failure to remove tools when job is complete
    c. Failure to lubricate
    d. Forgotten tools and parts

1. What are human factors and how can they affect aircraft maintenance operations?

<u>Chapter 14</u>

Human Factors

ANALYSIS
QUESTIONS

name:

date:

2. Define "human factors" as it relates to aircraft maintenance.

3. Human factors can be something in the work environment or internal to the AMT, but most are a combination. Name two human factors that affect AMTs that are the result of both external and internal causes. Describe the external and internal causes for each.

Chapter 14
Human Factors

ANALYSIS
QUESTIONS

name:

date:

4. Name three things you can do as an AMT to improve communication at your workplace.

5. Imagine you have been assigned a repair task and the information you have been given contradicts the steps that you mastered during training. To whom would you take this concern, and what would you say?

6. Many websites and programs provide helpful information on human factors and how it affects safety. Name two FAA sources and two other sources for information.